D1698460

DEUTSCHES
INSTITUT FÜR
STADT
BAU
KUNST

Herausgeber
Christoph Mäckler · Wolfgang Sonne [Deutsches Institut für Stadtbaukunst]

Konzeption und Koordination
Wolfgang Sonne

Grafische Gestaltung
Miriam Bussmann, Berlin

Lektorat
Kerstin Forster · Constanze Nobs · Wolfgang Sonne

Fotografien Vorwort
Detlef Podehl

Lithografie
Licht & Tiefe, Berlin

Druck
fgb freiburger graphische betriebe, Freiburg

DORTMUNDER VORTRÄGE ZUR STADTBAUKUNST **4**
DORTMUND LECTURES ON CIVIC ART

New Civic Art

CHRISTOPH MÄCKLER · WOLFGANG SONNE (HG.)   DEUTSCHES INSTITUT FÜR STADTBAUKUNST

Inhaltsverzeichnis / Content

Vorwort

Städtebau ist lokal – Wissenschaft ist international: Schon vor diesem Hintergrund ist es gerechtfertigt, sich am Deutschen Institut für Stadtbaukunst explizit mit neuen Forschungen zum Städtebau in Großbritannien und den USA zu beschäftigen. Im Zeitalter der Globalisierung erscheint dies geradezu als Selbstverständlichkeit – die es jedoch überraschenderweise nicht ist. Vieles ist noch unbekannt und vieles wird mit Vorurteilen betrachtet. Ja, wenn man den neugierigen und lebendigen Austausch anlässlich der vielen internationalen Städtebaukonferenzen um 1910 anschaut, so scheint es, dass trotz verbesserter Kommunikationswege und gesteigerter Informationsfülle heute international weniger gewusst wird als damals.

Um diesen Wissensaustausch zu befördern, fanden 2011 die vierten Dortmunder Vorträge zur Stadtbaukunst mit britischen und amerikanischen Experten statt, die neue Erkenntnisse und Konzepte auf dem Feld des Städtebaus aus Universitäten und Planungsinstitutionen vorstellten.

Harald Bodenschatz führte als einer der seinerzeit ersten ernsthaften Rezipienten des New Urbanism in Deutschland in die Veranstaltung ein und räumte mit einer Reihe von Missverständnissen auf, die den New Urbanism seit seiner Entstehung in den Achtzigerjahren in der deutschen Architektenschaft und Planerzunft begleiteten. Diese waren weitaus mehr von deutschen Diskurspositionen geprägt als von tatsächlichem Verständnis oder internationalem Weitblick.

Als Vertreter des Congress for the New Urbanism stellte Norman Garrick die Mobilitätsprinzipien des New Urbanism vor: Anstelle der autogerechten Stadt des American Sprawl legte er die Vielfalt der Verkehrsformen dar, die für eine urbane Mobilität berücksichtigt werden müssen, und stellte den Verkehr in ein angemessenes Verhältnis zu städtischen Räumen und anderen Funktionen. Grundsätzliche städtebauliche Strategien und nicht angeblich historistische Stilvorlieben wurden hier als das zentrale Anliegen des New Urbanism deutlich.

Für die Prince's Foundation for Community Building sprach Ben Bolgar. Er machte deutlich, dass der auf die nachhaltige Schaffung von Gemeinschaften abzielende Städtebau der Prince's Foundation weniger eine Frage des architektonischen Stils als vielmehr eine Frage eines grundlegenden kulturellen Verständnisses der Stadt und des Städtebaus ist. Für langfristig vielfältig nutzbare Stadtformen, vom Alltagsleben ihrer Bewohner ausgehend, erweist es sich als sinnvoll, von erprobten und bewährten Mustern auszugehen – eine Ansicht, für die der Prince of Wales von vielen Fachvertretern in den Achtzigerjahren belächelt wurde und für die er heute vielfach geachtet wird.

Drei Vorträge stellten neue Forschungen aus britischen Universitäten zum Städtebau vor. Matthew Carmona berichtete von den britischen Bestrebungen, städtebauliches Handeln über Gestaltungssatzungen zu regeln. Weit weniger aufgeregt als hierzulande, wo hinter jeder Regelung schon die Beschneidung der künstlerischen Freiheit gewittert wird, stehen Urban Design Codes in Großbritannien in einer Tradition der pragmatischen Konventionsbildung, mit der private und öffentliche Interessen in einen angemessenen Ausgleich gebracht werden sollen.

Michael Hebbert nahm die aktuelle Thematik des Klimaschutzes auf und brach sie auf den konkreten Stadtraum herunter: Sein Vortrag zur „Straßenatmosphäre" war keineswegs metaphorisch gemeint, sondern legte einen vergessenen Erkenntnisstrang einer urbanen Klimaforschung frei, der weitaus genauer und konkreter war als manche heutigen Zugänge zu Stadtbelüftung und Hitzeinseln. Insbesondere die Berücksichtigung auch klimatisch positiver Eigenschaften der im Namen der Hygiene lange verpönten Korridorstraße verspricht neue Zugänge zu diesem alten städtebaulichen Typus.

Sergio Porta untersuchte in seinem mit Ombretta Romice verfassten Vortrag die Eigenschaften eines auf der Parzelle aufbauenden Städtebaus. Während die Diskussion um Block oder Parzelle in Deutschland manchmal klassenkämpferische Züge annimmt, wurde in diesen auf Conzen und Rossi aufbauenden Forschungen zur Langzeitperformance der Parzelle deutlich, dass es sich um ein städtebauliches Grundelement handelt, das weitgehend unabhängig von sich wandelnden ökonomischen, politischen und sozialen Einflüssen existiert und in seiner flexiblen Kleinteiligkeit langfristigen Erfolg städtebaulicher Konfigurationen befördert.

Die hier abgedruckten vierten Dortmunder Vorträge zur Stadtbaukunst wurden am 9. Dezember 2011 im Rudolf-Chaudoire-Pavillon der TU Dortmund gehalten. Als neue Erkenntnisse zur Stadtbaukunst aus dem englischsprachigen Raum sind sie unter dem programmatischen Titel "New Civic Art" zusammengefasst.

PREFACE

The German Institute for Civic Art (Deutsches Institut für Stadtbaukunst) was founded in 2008 at the University of Technology in Dortmund (TU Dortmund). The major aim of the Institute is to recombine the diverse disciplines concerned with city development such as architecture, planning, transportation engineering, applied sociology, economic sciences etc. The term "civic art" (Stadtbaukunst) signifies two aspects: first, it underlines the design aspect in planning; second, it describes the art of bringing all diverse aspects of the city together.

The Dortmund Lectures on Civic Art (Dortmunder Vorträge zur Stadtbaukunst) are the major public lecture series of the Institute since 2008. This volume brings together leading experts in urban design from the UK and the US with new research. These approaches which are all characterised by an evidence based understanding of the city (instead of idealistic manifestoes) are subsumed under the programmatic heading "New Civic Art".

Dortmund, im Januar 2014
Die Herausgeber

1 Norman Garrick

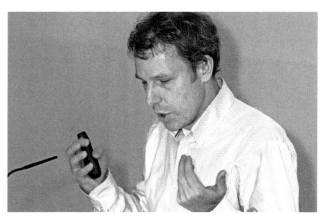

2 Matthew Carmona

3 Ben Bolgar

4 Sergio Porta

5 Alexander Pellnitz, Harald Bodenschatz, Christoph Mäckler

6 Michael Hebbert, Norman Garrick

Dortmunder Vorträge zur Stadtbaukunst
Dortmund Lectures on Civic Art

1 *New Urbanism – eine Antwort auf den US-amerikanischen sprawl.*

HARALD BODENSCHATZ *(Miss-)Verständnisse über den New Urbanism in Deutschland*

Stadt**Bauwelt**

12|00

31. Mai 2000 91. Jahrgang

New Urbanism ist ein bunter, ja schillernder Begriff, der kaum einzuhegen ist; er bezeichnet ein komplexes städtebauliches Phänomen, das in den Achtzigerjahren in den USA seinen Ausgang nahm: *New Urbanism* ist ein städtebauliches Programm, ein städtebauliches Netzwerk, ein städtebauliches Produkt.[1] Er ist eine Antwort auf die Entwicklung der US-amerikanischen Stadt, ein Programm zur Einflussnahme auf diese Entwicklung – unter den Bedingungen eines vornehmlich privaten Städtebaus. *New Urbanism* richtet sich nicht nur an Fachwelt und Politik, sondern auch an die Träger der städtebaulichen Entwicklung, an die neuen Mittelschichten, an zivilgesellschaftliche Initiativen und an die interessierte Immobilienwirtschaft. Die auf dem US-amerikanischen Markt relativ erfolgreichen, in der akademischen Welt aber umstrittenen städtebaulichen Produkte des *New Urbanism* werden auch weltweit nachgefragt und exportiert.

New Urbanism wird bei uns als neotraditionalistischer Kulissenzauber verspottet, in den USA hingegen als offene Debatte um eine zeitgemäße Städtebaureform verstanden. New Urbanism ist eine amerikanische Antwort auf Suburb, Edge City und Sprawl, kein Konzept, das auf europäische Städte übertragbar wäre.

2 Titel der vom Autor mitherausgegebenen Bauwelt 12/2000 zum Thema New Urbanism.

KRITIK AM *NEW URBANISM*

In Deutschland erregte der *New Urbanism* vor allem in den Jahren 2000 bis 2003 Aufmerksamkeit, danach wurde es merklich stiller. Die Kritik von Teilen der deutschen Fachwelt betraf vor allem zwei Aspekte: zum einen die Architektur, die traditionelle Architektur, die als nicht zeitgenössisch angesehen wurde, zum anderen die vermuteten sozialen Implikationen, wie die soziale Orientierung auf die Mittelschichten. Die erste Kritik wurde vor allem von Architekten, die zweite überwiegend von Stadtplanern kultiviert. Die Kritiker sahen den *New Urbanism* als ein typisches Produkt US-amerikanischer Unkultur, als Teil des generellen neoliberalen Trends, der sich in den USA durchgesetzt hatte und nun auf Europa überschwappte. Die meisten Verfasser dieser Kritik demonstrierten ein konsolidiertes Vorurteil, ohne dass ihnen das brei-

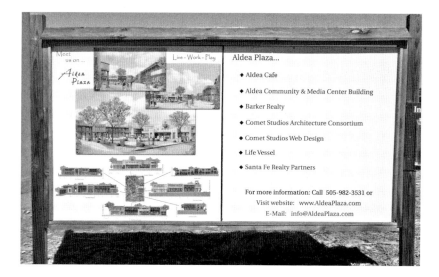

3 Aldea Plaza (New Mexico), geplant vom „Großvater" des New Urbanism Andres Duany: Werbetafel (oben), Infrastruktur noch ohne Bauten (Mitte) und erste Bauten (unten).

te Spektrum praktischer Beispiele wirklich vertraut war, ohne dass sie je an einem Kongress des *New Urbanism* teilgenommen haben, ohne dass sie über die aktuellen Debatten informiert waren und ohne dass sie die Organisationsformen kannten.

Am 11. Januar 2007 erschien ein Artikel des zu Recht hochgeschätzten Architekturjournalisten Gerhard Matzig in der *Süddeutschen Zeitung* mit dem Titel: „Alle Räder stehen still. Erst Feinstaub, jetzt Verkehrslärm – Die EU beerdigt den Moderne-Traum der autogerechten Stadt". Matzig meinte dabei das „unrühmliche Ende" zweier alter Träume der Moderne: nicht nur des Traums von der „autogerechten Stadt", sondern auch des Traums von einer „Vorstadt als Lebensraum im Gegensatz zur Stadt als Arbeitswelt". Aber was soll diesen beerdigten Träumen folgen? Matzig wurde hier sehr, sehr vorsichtig, nur eines wusste er sicher: „Städte mit Droschken, Hochrädern und Spazierstock-Flaneuren, wie sie der ,*New Urbanism*' vorschlägt, sind nicht die Antwort." Da haben wir es, dieses in der deutschen Fachdebatte immer noch irritierende Begriffspaar – *New Urbanism*, wo *New* für viele für alt zu stehen scheint. Und da haben wir auch die üblichen Reflexe, Vorurteile, Ängste, die immer noch mit diesem Begriffspaar verbunden sind. Für viele ist *New Urbanism* mit dem Bild einer Stadt von vorgestern verknüpft, wie es scheinbar in Seaside, der ersten neuen Kleinstadt des *New Urbanism*, zum Ausdruck kam. Seaside in Florida bündelt die emotionalen Reflexe in exemplarischer Form – offenbar auch diejenigen von Gerhard Matzig.

Solche Vorurteile zeichnen ein Zerrbild nicht nur des *New Urbanism*, sondern auch der US-amerikanischen Stadt. Sie unterschätzen sowohl die Dynamik der US-amerikanischen Stadt als auch die des *New Urbanism*. Das Bild von Stadt und Bewegung, das viele Kritiker entwerfen, ist hoffnungslos veraltet. All das bedeutet nicht, dass der *New Urbanism* nicht der Kritik bedürfe. Im Gegenteil. Hier ist manches zu kritisieren, ob gestalterisch, funktional, sozial oder hinsichtlich des Verkehrs, und das wird auch innerhalb des *New Urbanism* so gesehen. Die Kultur der Selbstkritik dort ist eine der Stärken, die wir in Europa oft vermissen.

Der in der weniger informierten deutschen Fachwelt gängige Blick auf die Städte in den USA ist durch ein relativ starres, wenig bewegliches Bild geprägt. Die US-amerikanische Stadt erscheint in dieser Optik kaputt, in *suburbia* aufgelöst, durch Autobahnen zerschnitten, ethnisch und sozial zerfallen, architektonisch ein Chaos, ohne jede politische und planerische Führung, dem privaten Kapital hilflos ausgeliefert. Detroit gilt als Musterbeispiel einer solchen Stadt. Mancher wird nun vielleicht sagen: Das Bild ist doch im Grundsatz richtig. Im Grundsatz, ja. Was das Bild aber ausklammert, sind die unübersehbaren Veränderungen, die die US-amerikanischen Städte seit den Siebzigerjahren erfahren haben, Veränderungen, die keineswegs vorrangig positiv sind, aber auch nicht nur negativ, sondern widersprüchlich. Das übliche Bild einer US-amerikanischen Stadt in Deutschland bezieht sich vor allem auf den Zustand der Stadtregionen in den Siebzigerjahren.

Seit den Siebzigerjahren haben sich sowohl *suburbia* als auch *downtown* räumlich wie sozial sehr stark verändert. Knapp zugespitzt heißt das: In den USA vollzog sich ein neuer Schub der Suburbanisierung, ein neuer Schub des *sprawl*, und gleichzeitig ein Prozess der Rezentralisierung, eine Renaissance der Stadtzentren. Wer vielleicht zwanzig Jahre nicht mehr in den USA war, würde sich heute über den Umbau der Zentren etwa von Chicago und Los Angeles sehr wundern. Wir erleben zurzeit, wie es Robert Fishman, ein Hochschullehrer im Umfeld des *New Urbanism*, schön beschrieben hat,[2] eine zugleich dezentralisierende wie rezentralisierende Entwicklung der US-amerikanischen Stadtregion. Beide Prozesse werden wesentlich von den Mittelschichten getragen, die jedoch nicht mehr die Mittelschichten der fordistischen Gesellschaft sind

MERKMALE DES *NEW URBANISM*

Noch vor zwanzig Jahren war *New Urbanism* in Deutschland nur wenigen Spezialisten ein Begriff: Wer hatte schon das Buch von Prinz Charles *A Vision of Britain* (1989) bis zum Schluss durchgeblättert, um

4 New Urbanism, von Prinz Charles vorgestellt: Seaside (Florida), abgebildet in: HRH The Prince of Wales, Die Zukunft unserer Städte, München 1990.

auf ein merkwürdiges neues Städtchen namens Seaside zu stoßen? Wer glaubte damals dem Prinzen, dass ausgerechnet dieses Städtchen „beginnt, das architektonische Denken überall in den Vereinigten Staaten zu beeinflussen"[3]? Wer hatte schon den US-Pavillon auf der Architekturbiennale in Venedig 1996, auf dem das neue Disney-Städtchen Celebration vorgestellt wurde, als fachlichen Beitrag ernst genommen? Die US-amerikanische Stadt schien wieder einmal ein Monster erzeugt zu haben – eine Kunststadt, ein gefährliches Gebräu von gestriger Architektur, sozialer Sterilität und Abgeschlossenheit. Der Film *The Truman Show*, der 1998 in Seaside gedreht wurde, hat dieses Bild hierzulande bekräftigt. Den Kritikern gilt *New Urbanism* seither als Disneyland, rückwärtsgewandt, hoffnungslos nostalgisch, ja mehr noch: als ein Vorgaukeln falscher Vergangenheit, als geschichtsfälschend. Doch ein solches Bild ist trügerisch, zu einfach, zu bequem. Der Ausgangspunkt des *New Urbanism* war gar nicht der nostalgische Kreuzzug gegen die moderne Architektur, sondern die Kritik an der Zersiedlung der US-amerikanischen Metropolregionen. Wichtigstes Ziel ist der Kampf gegen den *sprawl*, auch heute noch. Das hat noch gar nichts mit Architektur zu tun.

Doch was heißt das: Kampf gegen den *sprawl*? Das heißt vor allem, um in unserer Begrifflichkeit zu bleiben: Konversion, möglichst Wiedernutzung von Sied-

lungsflächen statt Neubau auf der grünen Wiese. Das heißt zum Beispiel: Revitalisierung von Stadtzentren. Der erste Revitalisierungsplan eines *New Urbanism*-Büros für ein verfallenes Großstadtzentrum wurde 1995 für Providence entwickelt, die Hauptstadt des kleinen Staates Rhode Island. In Providence fand im Jahr 2006 der 14. Kongress des *New Urbanism* statt, und der Umbau des Stadtzentrums war dabei ein zentrales Thema. Es geht aber auch um die neue Nutzung ehemaliger Industrieflächen, den sogenannten *brownfields*, ein Thema, mit dem wir in Europa sehr vertraut sind. In Milwaukee (Wisconsin) finden sich zu diesem Thema interessante Beispiele. Es geht um die neue Nutzung aufgegebener Shoppingcenter, sogenannter *greyfields*, ein wichtiges Aktionsfeld praktischer Konversionsprojekte, das uns in Europa noch sehr fremd ist. Ein bekanntes Beispiel hierfür ist The Crossings in Mountain View (Kalifornien). Wiedernutzung heißt weiter: Stärkung historischer Suburbs, nicht nur der schicken *railway*-Suburbs, die vor dem Ersten Weltkrieg entstanden sind, sondern vor allem der Suburbs aus der Zeit nach dem Zweiten Weltkrieg. Viele dieser Suburbs sind zurzeit die Verlierer der neuen Dynamik der US-amerikanischen Metropolregionen. *New Urbanism* schließt aber auch den Neu- und Umbau von Suburbs mit ein sowie eine Nachrüstung von Zentren in den besagten Wohngegenden. Ein Beispiel hierfür ist Haile Village Center bei Gainesville (Florida).

5 New Urbanism Disney-Stadt Celebration (Florida), vorgestellt auf der Architekturbiennale in Venedig 1996, Titel eines Faltblattes.

6 Transit Oriented Development Del Mar Station TOD: verdichtete Bebauung nach Plänen von Stefanos Polyzoides, einem der Väter des New Urbanism, an einem Vorort-Bahnhof in Pasadena (Kalifornien), 2003.

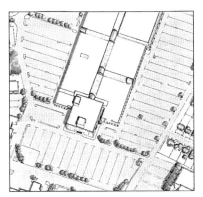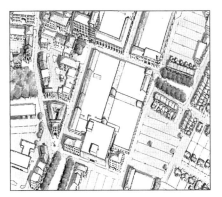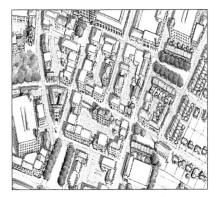

7 Greyfields into Goldfields: Konversion aufgegebener Shoppingcenter nach den Prinzipien des New Urbanism am Beispiel der Eastgate Mall in Chatanooga (Tennessee). Links 1997, Mitte „heute" (2001) und rechts in einer möglichen Zukunft, Dover Kohl & Partners.

Der Kampf gegen *sprawl* heißt also nicht: Kampf gegen *suburbia* überhaupt. Das ist oft ein großes Missverständnis, ein solcher Kampf wäre völlig unrealistisch. *Suburbia* ist keine Erfindung der Nachkriegszeit, sondern war immer Teil der Entwicklung der US-amerikanischen Stadt, natürlich auch der europäischen Stadt. Ziel des *New Urbanism* ist eine andere Form von Suburbs: baulich dichter, stärker nutzungsgemischt, sozial vielfältig, fußgängerorientiert und gut mit anderen Orten der Metropolregionen verbunden.

Und die Architektur, spielt sie denn überhaupt keine Rolle? Natürlich spielt sie eine wichtige Rolle. Stilistisch ist der *New Urbanism* aber nicht festgelegt, es finden sich dort Vertreter traditioneller wie moderner Baustile. Wichtiger als der Stil ist die Betonung der Besonderheit des Ortes. Auffällig ist bei den Projekten des *New Urbanism* jedenfalls die Dominanz des Städtebaus über die Architektur. Grundlage eines Projekts ist der *Masterplan*, der den Stadtgrundriss sowie die Verteilung der öffentlichen und privaten Grundstücke und Bauten festlegt. Zusätzlich gibt es einen *urban code*, ein städtebauliches Regelwerk, das die architektonische Gestaltung bestimmt. Erarbeitet werden diese planerischen Grundlagen oft durch ein besonderes Verfahren, *charrette* genannt. Dabei kommen die Planer mit den Bauherren, Vertretern öffentlicher Institutionen, gesellschaftlicher Gruppen und weiteren Zuständigen zusammen, um im Laufe einiger Tage stufenweise die Planung zu erarbeiten. *Masterplan*, *urban code* und *charrette* bilden das Instrumentarium des *New Urbanism*. Es erzwingt von vorneherein eine Zusammenschau von städtebaulicher, landschaftsplanerischer und architektonischer Planung.

Das ist das Ziel, die Realität freilich ist weit bescheidener. Das vielleicht wichtigste sozialräumliche Prinzip des *New Urbanism* ist die Ablehnung selbst gewählter Ghettos (*gated communities*) und die Befürwortung der maximalen Verknüpfung einer Siedlung mit dem Umfeld. Viele Beispiele kommen diesem Ziele nahe – die meisten, aber keineswegs alle. Es gibt auch auf dem Gebiet des *New Urbanism* Architek-

ten, die den programmatischen Prinzipien des *New Urbanism* in ihrer Praxis widersprechen. Dazu gehören nicht nur einige wenige *gated communities*, sondern auch neue Suburbs, die etwa nur durch eine einzige Zugangsstraße erschlossen werden und daher exklusiv wirken. Allerdings ist die Disneystadt Celebration keine *gated community*, wie immer wieder in Deutschland behauptet wird.

Nehmen wir einen weiteren Aspekt: die soziale Vielfalt. Diese beschränkt sich in der Regel auf ein gewisses Spektrum innerhalb der Mittelschichten selbst, ein Spektrum, das angesichts des privaten Städtebaus in den USA nur schwer zu erweitern ist. Gerade der Erfolg von *New Urbanism*-Projekten hatte sich in der Vergangenheit auch in steigenden Immobilienpreisen niedergeschlagen. Und die Forderung nach hochwertigen Baumaterialien – etwa Holz statt Plastik als Fassadendekor – hat ihren Preis. Betrachtet man aber die Spanne der Kaufpreise für Wohnungen in einem städtebaulichen Projekt als Indikator für eine gewisse soziale Vielfalt, so ist diese bei *New Urbanism*-Projekten oft größer als bei Projekten in Deutschland. Das galt in besonderem Maße für Celebration.

Das anspruchsvollste Ziel des *New Urbanism* ist aber auf einer anderen räumlichen Stufenleiter verortet: auf der Ebene der Region. Nur auf regionaler Ebene, so die Einschätzung zumindest eines Teils der Bewegung des *New Urbanism*, können soziale wie räumliche Ziele nachhaltig durchgesetzt werden. Ziel ist eine vernetzte, sozial ausbalancierte *regional city* mit flexiblen Wachstumsgrenzen. Ein Protagonist dieser Auffassung ist Peter Calthorpe, der zusammen mit William Fulton im Jahr 2001 ein Manifest zu dieser Thematik veröffentlicht hat: das Buch *The Regional City. Planning for the End of Sprawl*. Natürlich gibt es innerhalb der Bewegung Streit darüber, wo die Schwerpunkte gesetzt werden sollen – aber es geht immer um die Schwerpunktsetzung, nicht um ein Entweder-oder. Die in Deutschland immer noch erlebbare unproduktive Konfrontation von Vertretern der europäischen Stadt und Vertretern der Zwischenstadt ist mit Blick auf das

Programm des *New Urbanism* völlig unsinnig: Kommt es doch nicht darauf an, die kompakte Stadt auf Kosten der zersiedelten Stadt zu retten oder umgekehrt. Vielmehr ist eine Perspektive gefragt, die die Qualifizierung der gesamten Stadtregion in den Blick nimmt — die kompakte Stadt und die Zwischenstadt.

New Urbanism ist aber nicht nur eine städtebauliche Produktpalette, die man bewundern oder kritisieren kann. Er ist auch eine Institution, eine institutionalisierte Bewegung. Er organisiert sich — in bewusster kritischer Anlehnung an die Kongresse für Neues Bauen (CIAM) der Zwischenkriegszeit — in Form von Kongressen (*Congress for the New Urbanism CNU*). 1993 fand in Alexandria (Virginia) der erste Kongress statt. Der 21. Kongress fand 2013 zum Thema Living Community in Salt Lake City statt. Der Congress of the *New Urbanism* ist keine Kaderorganisation, sondern ein relativ offenes Netzwerk, das durch eine kleine Gruppe gesteuert wird. Ein Netzwerk, das sich jedes Jahr einmal auf einem Kongress mit etwa gut tausend Teilnehmern trifft. Auf den Kongressen begegnen sich Leute, die in Europa erst gar nicht miteinander sprechen würden: Vertreter der behutsamen Stadterneuerung, neotraditionalistische Architekten, hochrangige Politiker, Developer, Architekturkritiker, Umweltaktivisten und Vertreter sozialer Stadtteilinitiativen. Vor diesem Hintergrund gibt es Vertreter ganz unterschiedlicher programmatischer Strömungen, die sich gegenseitig mit ihrer Perspektive nerven, aber auch befruchten. Diese Begegnung unterschiedlicher Akteure ist einer der faszinierendsten Aspekte des *New Urbanism*. Ein solches buntes Spektrum im Rahmen einer groben Zielsetzung spiegelt eine zivilgesellschaftliche Kultur wider, die Europa oft fehlt. Eine Kultur, die keiner einzelnen Partei verpflichtet ist.

Die Teilnehmer der Kongresse werden automatisch für ein Jahr Mitglieder des *Congress for the New Urbanism*, also Mitglieder des Netzwerks. Als solche erhalten sie eine Art Mitgliedszeitschrift, die *New Urban News*, eine erstaunlich nüchterne, unaufgeregte Zeitschrift, die neue Projekte, Debatten, aber auch ausführlich Kritiken vorstellt. Aus europäischer Sicht ist die Kultur der selbstkritischen Verarbeitung wichtiger städtebaulicher Projekte durchaus eindrucksvoll. Die Prinzipien des *New Urbanism* sind in einer Charta zusammengefasst, die 1996 auf dem vierten *Congress for the New Urbanism* in Charleston (South Carolina) verabschiedet wurde. Auf Deutsch wurde diese Charta in der Zeitschrift *Die alte Stadt* 4/1998 publiziert. Ende 1999 erschien ein Buch, offiziell herausgegeben vom Congress for the *New Urbanism*, das die Charta ausführlich erläuterte. Später wurde die Charta durch ein Regelwerk zu nachhaltiger Architektur und nachhaltigem Städtebau ergänzt.[4]

Der Congress for the *New Urbanism* ist also kein Berufsverband, kein Verband von Architekten und Planern, sondern ein überberuflicher Zusammenschluss, eine programmatische Institution. In dieser Hinsicht ist er auch komplexer als die historischen Kongresse für Neues Bauen (CIAM). In Europa finden wir professionelle Organisationen, aber auch Kaderorganisationen aller Art, mit allzu festem Programm, und jeder kleine Abweichler wird ausgeschlossen oder weggegrault. Das ist oft noch eine Schwäche europäischer zivilgesellschaftlicher Initiativen. *New Urbanism* ist vor allem ein Netzwerk zum Austausch und zur Propagierung einer Reform des Städtebaus. Dieses Netzwerk ist wiederum mit anderen Netzwerken verknüpft, die ähnliche Ziele verfolgen: etwa mit Smart Growth America, Sierra Club, National Trust for Historic Preservation, National Neighborhood Coalition und vielen mehr. Kooperiert wird auch mit dem Urban Land Institute, einer einflussreichen Stiftung der Immobilienwirtschaft. Diese flexible Organisationsform ist eine wichtige Voraussetzung für erfolgreiche Öffentlichkeitsarbeit.

PROGRAMMATISCHE DYNAMIK DES *NEW URBANISM*

Während in Deutschland viele Fachleute gebannt oder geschockt auf einige ausgewählte architektonische

8 Titel des grundlegenden Buches The Regional City. Planning for the End of Sprawl von Peter Calthorpe und William Fulton, 2001.

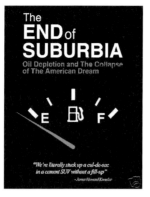

9 DVD The End of Suburbia, ein New Urbanism Propaganda-film von James Howard Kunstler aus dem Jahre 2004.

Produkte der *New Urbanists* schauten, entwickelte sich die Debatte innerhalb des *New Urbanism* gegensätzlich zu jeglichem Architekturstreit. Ein wichtiges Thema waren schon um 2004 strategische Überlegungen zum Abbau der Abhängigkeit vom Öl in einer Zeit teurer Energie, eine Aufgabe, die – so die Überzeugung der *New Urbanists* – unsere Zukunft prägen wird. An der breit gestreuten Propaganda-DVD *The End of Suburbia* hat ein Enfant terrible des *New Urbanism* mitgewirkt, der Schriftsteller James Howard Kunstler. Ausdruck dieser Entwicklung ist auch der Aufstieg von Douglas Farr in die Führungsriege des *New Urbanism*, der 2008 ein Standardwerk zum nachhaltigen Städtebau veröffentlichte: *Sustainable Urbanism. Urban Design with Nature.*

In der Tat gewinnt das Thema Umwelt ein immer größeres Gewicht innerhalb des *New Urbanism*. Interessantestes Zeugnis dieser Entwicklung ist der Versuch, eine Art Zertifikat für guten, umweltgerechten Städtebau zu entwickeln. Dieser Versuch hat einen Namen: LEED-ND, Leadership in Energy and Environmental Design for Neighborhood Developments. Douglas Farr war an diesem Versuch maßgeblich beteiligt. LEED-ND war zunächst ein auf Gebäude bezogenes ökologisches Zertifikatssystem, das nunmehr auch auf den Städtebau ausgedehnt wird. Zu diesem Zwecke arbeiten der U.S. Green Building Council, der Natural Resource Defense Council und der Congress for the *New*

Urbanism zusammen. Der Green Building Council ist ein Zusammenschluss von umweltorientierten Vertretern der Bauindustrie, Natural Resource Defense Council ist eine der einflussreichsten US-amerikanischen Umweltorganisationen. Ziel dieser drei Organisationen ist es, eine Art Rating samt Label zu kreieren, das auf bestehende und neue städtebauliche Produkte angewandt werden kann. Wichtige Kriterien sind etwa bauliche Dichte, Nähe zum öffentlichen Nahverkehr, Mischnutzung, Vielfalt an Gebäudetypen sowie Fußgängerfreundlichkeit. Dieses Beispiel zeigt, wie der *Congress for the New Urbanism* mit zahlreichen anderen Netzwerken zusammenarbeitet, und dass gerade diese Verknüpfung von Netzwerken eine erfolgreiche Lobby- und Öffentlichkeitsarbeit ermöglicht.

New Urbanism ist daher nicht nur wegen seiner konkreten Produkte von Interesse, sondern auch wegen seiner Organisations- und Arbeitsform, seiner Dynamik, seiner erfolgreichen Versuche, die Grenzen der Fachdisziplinen zu überschreiten. *New Urbanism* ist ein äußerst komplexes Phänomen, das durch ein paar Bilder nicht zu erklären ist, und das durch ein paar Bilder auch nicht zu erschlagen ist.

NEW URBANISM UND EUROPA?

Brauchen wir auch in Europa eine Städtebaureform-Bewegung? Sind unsere Städte nicht in einem viel besseren Zustand als die Städte der USA? Das mag ja sein, aber das heißt nicht, dass wir uns zurücklehnen können. Die Entwicklung unserer Städte ist in dreifacher Hinsicht bedrohlich: Räumlich fördert sie trotz aller Sonntagsreden weiter die Zersiedelung der Landschaft, sozial fördert sie die Isolierung und das Auseinanderleben unterschiedlicher sozialer Schichten, und ökologisch ist sie weiterhin Energie verschwendend und wenig nachhaltig. Der Begriff Stadt selbst ist hohl geworden: Er weckt bilderbuchhafte Assoziationen, die mit der Realität nur noch wenig zu tun haben. Wir haben es nicht mehr mit Städten zu tun, sondern mit Großstadtregionen, mit denen wir noch keine festen Bilder verbinden.

Natürlich gibt es auch in Europa gewichtige städtebauliche Institutionen, Verbände, Propheten, Konzepte, Bücher und viele Projekte, die sich mit diesen Grundsatzfragen auseinandersetzen. Bekannte Vertreter der europäischen Städtebaudebatte sind etwa Léon und Rob Krier, aber auch Pier Luigi Cervellati, Thomas Sieverts und Richard Rogers. All diese Fachleute sprechen sich vehement gegen den *sprawl* aus, wenngleich ihre Konsequenzen sehr unterschiedlich sind. Doch diese Unterschiede werden leider nicht in einem konstruktiven Streit diskutiert, sondern in einem Krieg feindlicher Lager verklärt oder verdammt. Dabei geht es oft weniger um städtebauliche Positionen als um die architektonische Haltung: für oder gegen traditionalistische Architektur. Hinter dem dominanten, harten Architekturkrieg entfalten sich weitere, auch städtebauliche Konfliktfronten – etwa in Deutschland die Front zwischen den Vertretern der europäischen Stadt und der Zwischenstadt. Kennzeichen dieser Lager- und Frontenbildung ist ihre eindimensionale Enge: Sie ist ein Produkt der Profession, des Kampfes um kulturelle Hegemonie in der Architekturdebatte und letztendlich des Kampfes um Aufträge, kein Produkt einer breiten gesellschaftlichen Auseinandersetzung.

Was in Europa ebenfalls sehr unterentwickelt ist, ist die Evaluation von städtebaulichen Schlüsselprojekten. Wo finden wir Studien, die etwa die Sanierung des historischen Zentrums von Bologna in den Siebzigerjahren, die Produkte der Internationalen Bauausstellung Berlin 1984/87 oder die Anfang der Neunzigerjahre neu gestalteten öffentlichen Räume in Barcelona nüchtern verarbeiten? Vorherrschend ist eine kurzatmige Rezeption: Zu Beginn dieser Projekte wurde die Fachöffentlichkeit sowie die Öffentlichkeit mit euphorischen Berichten überschwemmt, während die distanzierte Betrachtung ihrer längerfristigen Brauchbarkeit unterblieb. Das ist einer nachhaltigen Städtebaukultur alles andere als zuträglich!

Die städtebaulichen Debatten an den Universitäten und zwischen den zivilgesellschaftlichen Initiativen in Europa sind mehr oder minder isoliert, zersplittert, in den Fronten historischer Auseinandersetzungen gefangen. Verteufelung, Abwehr und Ausgrenzung, Mangel an Evaluation beherrschen die europäischen Debatten, der Dialog ist erstarrt, Plattformen für einen

10 Titel des grundlegenden Buches: Sustainable Urbanism: Urban Design with Nature von Douglas Farr, 2008.

11 Zertifikat für nachhaltigen Städtebau: LEED-ND. Kombination von Logos des Congress for the New Urbanism, Natural Resource Defense Council und U.S. Green Building Council.

Dialog sind begrenzt. Eine wichtige Rolle in Deutschland spielt die Nationale Stadtentwicklungspolitik, eine Initiative des Bundesministeriums für Verkehr, Bau und Stadtentwicklung. Der Hintergrund sind Aktivitäten auf europäischer Ebene, die 2007 in die „LEIPZIG CHARTA zur nachhaltigen europäischen Stadt" mündeten. Im Jahre 2012 entstand – fünf Jahre später – das „Memorandum STÄDTISCHE ENERGI-EN – Zukunftsaufgaben der Städte".[5] Trotz all dieser Anstrengungen fehlen übergreifende programmatische, überprofessioncllc, internationale Institutionen. Europa braucht daher ein eigenes, unabhängiges Städtebaureformnetzwerk, das keine Zweigstelle des US-amerikanischen *New Urbanism* ist. Das bedeutet programmatisch: Erweiterung der Debatte auf die Ebene der Stadtregion und Vernetzung der gestalterischen, politischen, ökonomischen, sozialen und ökologischen Diskurse. Das bedeutet vor allem: Erarbeitung eines Programms, das den Umgang mit dem schwierigen städtebaulichen Erbe des 20. Jahrhunderts regelt. Ebenso: Evaluation der bedeutenden neueren Schlüsselprojekte des europäischen Städtebaus. Das bedeutet auch: Erneuerung des Blicks auf die reichen historischen Erfahrungen des Städtebaus in Europa, die uns durch eine oft einseitige Baugeschichtsschreibung nur in verzerrter Form überliefert sind. Und schließlich: Aufbau einer programmatischen instituti-

onalisierten Plattform, die diesen Erfahrungsaustausch ermöglicht und fördert. Erst dann sind wir nicht nur untereinander, sondern auch über den Atlantik hinweg wirklich dialogfähig. Ein wichtiger Anker einer solchen Plattform ist bereits heute das Deutsche Institut für Stadtbaukunst, das allerdings mit Blick auf ein breites deutsches Netzwerk durchaus noch ausbaufähig ist. Ein weiterer Anker ist der *Council for European Urbanism*, der zwar programmatisch gut aufgestellt ist, dessen Netzwerkqualität aber noch Verbesserungen zulässt.[6]

Dass es in Deutschland in den letzten Jahren etwas stiller um den *New Urbanism* geworden ist, hat viele Gründe, nicht zuletzt die Turbulenzen des Finanzkapitals, die andere Themen in den Schatten gerückt haben. In der Tat ist es notwendig zu fragen, was die stark veränderten Rahmenbedingungen – die Finanzkrise, die Immobilienkrise, der fortschreitende Klimawandel, der Abschied von einer Zeit billigen Öls, die Aussichten auf eine veränderte, neue Mobilität, der weltweite Umbau der Wirtschaft, die fortschreitende soziale Polarisierung, um nur einige zu nennen, für den Städtebau in den USA, aber auch in Europa bedeuten. All das sind Herausforderungen, die mehr denn je transprofessionelle Zusammenarbeit und internationalen Erfahrungsaustausch erfordern.

12 Dokumentation der C.E.U.D. (Council for European Urbanism Deutschland) Tagung „10 Jahre Zwischenstadt – wie weiter?" in Sundern, 2007.

Fußnoten

1 Der Autor war bei der Rezeption des *New Urbanism* in Deutschland an vorderster Front beteiligt. Er konzipierte 2000 das damalige Themenheft der *Bauwelt* zum *New Urbanism* zusammen mit dem Chefredakteur Felix Zwoch, das die US-amerikanische Städtebaubewegung erstmals einer breiteren Fachwelt in Deutschland ohne Polemik vorstellte: „New Urbanism. Städtebaureform auf Amerikanisch" *Bauwelt* 12/2000. Er verfasste zahlreiche Artikel und Vorträge an unterschiedlichen Universitäten zum *New Urbanism*, zwölf Vorträge allein im Jahr 2000, drei 2001 und vier 2002. 2004 veröffentlichte er zusammen mit Barbara Schönig das Buch *Smart Growth – New Urbanism – Liveable Communities. Programm und Praxis der Anti-Sprawl-Bewegung in den USA*.

2 Robert Fishman, „Beyond Sprawl. The New American Metropolis", in: Lars Bölling, Thomas Sieverts (Hrsg.), *Mitten am Rand. Auf dem Weg von der Vorstadt über die Zwischenstadt zur regionalen Stadtlandschaft*, Wuppertal 2004, S. 170 – 173

3 HRH The Prince of Wales, *Die Zukunft unserer Städte. Eine ganz persönliche Auseinandersetzung mit der modernen Architektur*, München 1990, S. 143

4 Vgl. www.cnu.org/sites/files/Canons.pdf

5 Die Leipzig Charta ist dokumentiert in: www.bmvbs.de/cae/servlet/contentblob/34480/publicationFile/518/ leipzig-charta-zur-nachhaltigen-europaeischen-stadt-angenommen-am-24-mai-2007.pdf, das Memorandum ist dokumentiert in: www.bmvbs.de/cae/servlet/content-blob/92098/publicationFile/65462/staedtische-energien-memorandum-de.pdf

6 Zum Council for European Urbanism vgl. www.ceunet.org. Zum Council for European Urbanism Deutschland vgl. http://de.ceunet.org

Abbildungsnachweise
Abb. 1, 3: Harald Bodenschatz, 2008
Abb. 2: *Bauwelt*, 12/2000
Abb. 4: HRH The Prince of Wales, *Die Zukunft unserer Städte*, München 1990
Abb. 5: Faltblatt
Abb. 6: Moule & Polyzoides Architects and Urbanists, *Work in Progress 2/3*, Pasadena 2003
Abb. 7: Congress for the New Urbanism, *Greyfields into Goldfields*, Ausgabe Juni 2001
Abb. 8: Peter Calthorpe und William Fulton, *The Regional City. Planning for the End of Sprawl*, 2001
Abb. 9: James Howard Kunstler, *The End of Suburbia*, DVD, 2004
Abb. 10: Douglas Farr, *Sustainable Urbanism. Urban Design with Nature*, 2008
Abb. 12 Council for European Urbanism Deutschland

1 Seaside, Florida; Founded: 1981, Designed by Andrés Duany and Elizabeth Plater-Zyberg

NORMAN GARRICK *Transportation and the Art of Placemaking in America*

1 During the second half of the 20th Century and early into the 21st Century, place-making in America has been characterized by a fragmented, monochromatic pattern where residential areas were separated from commercial areas which, in turn, were often separated from civic facilities. In 1981, the small resort town of Seaside was built on the Florida panhandle as the first complete mixed-use community in America in several decades. Seaside was such a radical concept for the time that it spawned the 'new urbanism' movement which developed around the idea of using Seaside as a template for future urban development in America.

2 The town center in Seaside is reminiscent of an older approach to place-making in America, with buildings oriented to streets rather than to parking lots, a town green, and mixed use buildings – mostly retail at ground level and some housing in the upper floors. In addition, the town center is full integrated with the surrounding residential neighborhoods, to which it is connected by a dense network of walkable streets. This is another break from the prevailing pattern of place making.

3 Residential Streets in Seaside, Florida, are characterized by a return to a much narrower carriageway, low speeds for vehicles, and beautiful design. All the streets are part of a dense and connected network – there are no cul-de-sacs.

2

3

4

4 This picture gives another view of the Seaside town center, with a glimpse of one of the community churches in the background. One of the most interesting features of the Seaside town center is that it was not built in its current form as a fully formed entity, but rather was based on the idea that it would evolve over time. Many businesses in Seaside were first incubated in temporary structures in the town. Once they proved economically viable they were moved into four story, mixed use buildings that were constructed as the funds became available with the increasing success of the community. Some of the more modest buildings from the early days of the town center have been repurposed and moved to less central locations. For example, a few of the older town center structures are now being used as classroom buildings for the expanding educational activities in Seaside.

5 The above picture shows from left: Andres Duany, CNU Founder and Architect; Scott Polikov, CNU Board Member and Town Planner; Peter Swift, Transportation Engineer; Norman Garrick, CNU Board Member and Professor of Civil Engineering.

5 Today the Congress for the New Urbanism is seen as the leading organization promoting walkable, mixed-use community development in America and internationally. According to the Charter of the CNU the goal is "*The restoration of existing urban centers and towns within coherent metropolitan regions, the reconfiguration of sprawling suburbs into communities of real neighborhoods and diverse districts, the conservation of natural environments, and the preservation of our built legacy*". One of the hallmarks of CNU, which sets it apart from most organizations working on the built environment, is its multidisciplinary approach to design, planning, policy and community involvement.

6 Many books have documented the conventional approach to place making in contemporary America. This book by Dolores Hayden and Jim Welk uses aerial photographs to illustrate the various patterns that populate the American landscape. In the next few pages we have included some of the images from this book to illustrate the extent to which Seaside and new urbanism differ from this conventional approach. The conventional approach is characterized by being almost completely automobile focused. As such, it is under increased strain because of a host of social, environmental, and, in particular, economical limits, that are beginning to become more obvious to the general public.

7 Over the last 50 years, thousands of huge shopping malls have been built in America. Today much of America's retail trade is conducted in this type of setting. The arrangement shown here is typical, with the mall building surrounded by parking and totally isolated from the surrounding residential area. In this environment, walking as a means of getting from one's home to the mall is difficult, if not impossible,

in many cases. Ironically, many malls have become popular as places where people DRIVE to in order to go WALKING, primarily for exercise. This is because much of the built landscape in America is so hostile to people on foot. More and more researchers are beginning to document a strong link between the nature of the built environment and the obesity crisis in America.

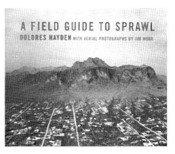

6

7

8 This image shows the type of single family home
that was typically constructed in many American suburbs prior to the financial crash of 2008. These types
of houses are sometimes referred to as snout houses –
because of the car garages that totally dominate the
front facade of the building.

8

9 Most major roads in American cities and suburban areas are littered with this pattern of strip development. The whole environment has been conceived for convenient access by cars. Any design for pedestrians is an afterthought – that is, if they are considered at all. In most places like this, people on foot are looked on with suspicion – either they are seen as vagrants or, at best, as people with an unreliable car that has broken down.

9

10 This image shows massive single family houses on a cul-de-sac in what was once farm land. Houses like this are sometimes referred to as MacMansions because of their sheer size and lack of a coherent style.

10

11 This image shows an isolated, single-use residential pod. This is the unit of development in many places in the American suburbs and increasingly in some American cities. Each pod is not only isolated from schools, retail and commercial uses, but also from other neighboring residential pods. As a result, almost every trip requires the use of a car. Often the only people on foot in this environment are joggers or dog walkers. My research team at the University of Connecticut has documented some of the problems associated with using this pattern as the building block of communities. These problems include much higher traffic fatalities, little walking or biking, and the resulting health problems associated with a more sedentary pattern of living.

11

12

13 Charleston, SC, founded 1690

14

15

12 This image shows a residential pod with a golf course as the community focus. Interestingly, although a common critique of modern American settlement is that they are not dense enough, in fact, in many places the density within the settlement itself is higher than would be expected and certainly as high as that in 1920s residential neighborhoods in many American cities. The reason this neighborhood is so car dependent is not due to the density, but rather due to the lack of mixed use development and the lack of an interconnected street system.

13 Contemporary patterns of development in America, as illustrated in the preceding images, represent a sharp break from the past. This map of Charleston, South Carolina is indicative of the approach to place making that prevailed in America up until about 1930. This picture illustrates how different the old pattern is when compared to the contemporary pattern. The dense, integrated street network is one of the most important characteristics of older American settlements and it is one that the Congress for the New Urbanism advocates that we return to.

14 This is Church Street in Charleston, South Carolina, showing the old pattern of American cities at street level. This relationship between building and street is no longer adhered to in many contemporary situations. In addition, features such as on-street parking are now eschewed. Also, design subtlety such as the terminated vista of the church and the details on the buildings are not part of the vocabulary of architecture or planning in most modern American town making. But these features are essential, as they create an environment that celebrates walking and slows down the cars, making it safer for walking. This pattern of community design (but not necessarily the architectural style) is an important tenet of new urbanism.

15 A second street view in Charleston showing the use of the street as a comfortable shared space. 'Shared space' is a term of art that was coined in Europe to describe a new philosophy for the design of streets and other public places in such a way that these places can be comfortably shared by different types of users with little or no need for regulations and rules. The Dutch engineer, Hans Monderman, is widely credited with popularizing the use of shared space in modern design. But as this picture shows, shared space is not new — it draws on an older tradition of design that was practiced all over the world.

16 The Beginning: Ford's Model T

16 The debut of Henry Ford's model T in 1908 signaled the start of the Automobile Era in America and eventually led to radical changes in how we build places. Not only did we change how we built new places, but we also modified existing cities to better accommodate cars. Cities like Charleston, South Carolina, were the exception to this rule, in that it managed to hold on to its pre-automobile character in the core of the city.

17 Vehicle miles traveled is one measure of the use and dominance of motorized vehicles in a culture. In the case of the United States, VMT started to rise with the debut of the Ford Model T in 1908, since cars were suddenly affordable to the average family. Between 1908 and the start of World War 2, VMT increased at a steady clip in America. After the war ended the growth of VMT resumed, but at a much accelerated rate, until it peaked at around 3 trillion miles in 2004. The post World War 2 growth in VMT in the USA was unmatched in the rest of the industrialized world. By 2004, the VMT per capita in the US was much higher than in any other country in the world. This discrepancy is partly due to the drastic changes in place-making in the USA after 1950.

The explosion in vehicle use in America after 1950 is a fascinating phenomenon that, among other influences, has changed the face of the country. But in many ways this explosion would not have been possible without a change in how we built places and how we modified existing places to better accommodate cars.

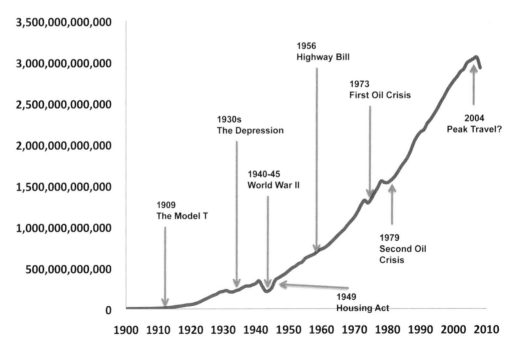

17 Vehicle Miles Traveled (in America)

18 Another way of looking at the explosion in motorized vehicle use in America is to consider the amount of miles driven per person, which increased by a factor of 5 between 1946 and 2004. By 2004, when this number peaked, the average number of miles driven in America for every man, woman and child was an almost hard-to-fathom 30 miles per day (50 kilometers per day). Many of the most serious issues of sustainability (for example, climate change and energy insecurity) that we face both in America and globally are in part a result of how much we drive in America.

19 The 1920s was a tumultuous period in urban planning. This was a time when technologies such as electricity, automobiles and airplanes were just beginning to be widely adopted, transforming how we lived and how we traveled — it was a time when the common belief was that we had broken with the past. This was also a period when there was great dissatisfaction with the character and the quality of life in cities. Out of this foment emerged dramatically new ideas about how urban places should be designed. One of the most significant voices calling for change was the Swiss born architect, Le Corbusier, who offered the vision of a new type of city which he dubbed 'The Radiant City'. Le Corbusier described the Radiant City in this way: *"We have allotted the entire ground surface of the city to the pedestrians. And since our apartment houses are all up in the air, raised on pilotis, it will be possible to walk across the city in any direction".*

20 The term 'The Modernist City' was also used to refer to a new urban prototype. The plan in this image, which was never implemented for central London, shows in some detail how the Modernist City was designed to function. One of the central tenets of the Modernist City was the idea of segregation. In this case, motorized movement was separated from pedestrians on different levels. Interestingly, although Le Corbusier supported the separation of pedestrians from vehicle traffic, he also railed against the particular configuration of separation shown here. Le Corbusier's idea was that the ground plan should be given over to the pedestrians, and the second level to cars. In practice, neither solution has worked well in cities.

18 Driving to Exhaustion: 1946: The average American drove 6 miles every day; 2004: The average American drove 30 miles per day

19 A New Vision – The Radiant City: Streets are an obsolete notion. There ought not to be such thinks as streets; we have to create something that will replace them. (Le Corbusier, The Radiant City, 1933)

20

21 This is a sketch of what the center of Zurich would have looked like, based on a conceptual plan to level the old city and replace it with a version of Le Corbusier's Radiant City. Plans of these kinds for various European cities were not uncommon. For the most part these ideas were not implemented in western Europe, except in some instances where war ravaged center cities were reconstructed or in some edge cities. In America, on the other hand, a massive amount of urban clearance was carried out, and many old style cities replaced with some version of the modernist city.

22 As part of the proposed reconstruction of the old city in Zurich, the medieval pattern of small, interconnected streets would have been replaced with a rationalized network of streets that would better accommodate automobile travel. This plan was rejected – and today Zurich's old town is the most beloved quarter in the city.

21

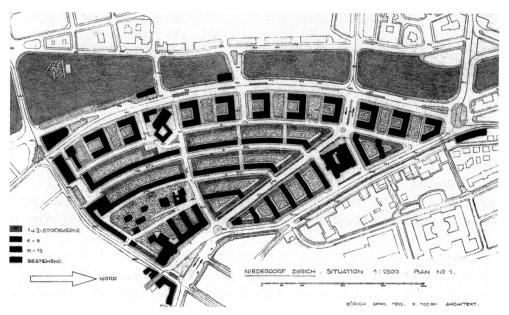

22

23

23 Plans for reconstructing cities in line with modernist thinking were not limited to North American or European cities. This is a view of King Street, Kingston, Jamaica, the main street of the old colonial city. This street is still largely intact, if somewhat down at heel. In the late 1960s, plans were drawn up to revitalize commercial Kingston by razing the wharves and other waterfront buildings and replacing them with modernist skyscrapers.

24 This picture shows the fruition of plans for remaking the waterfront area of Kingston. The buildings that formed this plan, which were largely completed by the early 1970s, never had the intended effects of revitalizing downtown Kingston. Like many projects of its time, it was never fully integrated within the existing fabric of the city and was mostly devoid of any street life or vitality. This area also lacks the fine grained, human quality that characterizes much of the rest of Kingston. The end result is that the Kingston waterfront is totally lacking in street level human activity – people on foot seem to avoid it like the plague. This is particularly ironic in this hot tropical city where the waterfront offers significant relief from the heat.

24

25 Hartford 1953

26 Hartford 1965

25 In America, modernism has left its mark in a dramatic way on a number of mid-sized cities in the northeast. One such case is Hartford, Connecticut, which used federal funds to essentially erase this neighborhood. In 1953, when this picture was taken, this was largely an Italian neighborhood that was considered a ghetto with deteriorating buildings. But it was also a tightly-knit community that was just a few blocks east of Main Street and the commercial heart of the city.

26 By 1962, Front Street was no more and had been replaced by Constitution Plaza, an almost perfect evocation of the Modernist city. This picture shows the new, shiny Constitution Plaza from the same vantage point as the previous picture of Front Street. Constitution Plaza erased not only buildings, but also the network of small streets which served as the basic building blocks for the neighborhood. It was not just a question of building style but that the very essence of the neighborhood was lost as the small, individually owned and mixed use buildings were replaced by monolithic buildings on a much larger scale. This area of town was converted into what is essentially an office park which was conveniently designed for the speedy and convenient flow of cars into and out of the massive parking garage which forms the foundation for the whole complex. During the day the offices are occupied, but the streets are largely devoid of people, and at night the whole complex goes to sleep. Most tragic for the city of Hartford was the loss of the people who lived in Front Street, an important community contributing to the liveliness of the downtown.

27 Urban renewal was just one of the many assaults on the integrity and structure of American cities during the middle of the 20th century. This picture of Hartford, Connecticut, from the 1930s shows a largely intact downtown with a network of relatively small streets and a dense fabric of mid-size and small buildings. In this picture, the area that is now Constitution Plaza is in the south-east quadrant – just west of the Connecticut River and south of the street that connects to the one bridge across the river.

28 This aerial of Hartford is from the 1960s, and compared to the earlier 1930s aerial, it is hard to recognize it as the same city. We can see the changes wrought by the construction of Constitution Plaza, with the dense, small scale urban fabric in the south eastern quadrant replaced by much larger buildings and by superblocks. But we can also see that the city is now bisected by two freeways – both of which have resulted in the removal of even more buildings and have fragmented the city. In one case, the freeway cuts off access to the river and in the second case it isolates the downtown from the residential north end. It is interesting to note that the area north of the freeway that appears to be a wasteland in this image has largely that same aspect to this day, more than 50 years later.

27

28

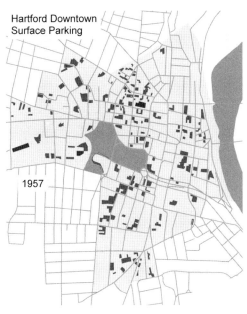

Hartford Downtown
Surface Parking

1957

29

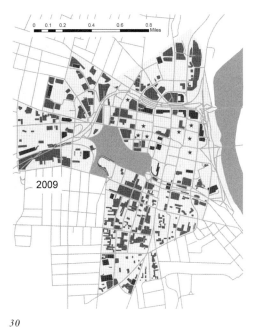

0   0.1   0.2   0.4   0.6   0.8
Miles

2009

30

29 Another element that has contributed to the loss of urban fabric in Hartford is parking. This image shows surface parking in red and garage parking in maroon for the year 1957.

30 This image shows the growing impact of parking in downtown Hartford. By 2009, parking lots and parking garages occupied well over 20% of the land area in downtown Hartford. This represented a growth in parking spaces from 15,000 to 45,000 spaces bet-ween 1957 and 2009. Shockingly, parking provision tripled while the city was losing population and bare-ly growing in terms of the number of jobs. One con-sequence of the changes in the land use pattern that we have discussed earlier was that they encouraged and facilitated more driving and less walking for transportation. This in turn leads to the need for much more parking for each person living or working in the city.

31 Another important influence in changing how we built places in America in the latter half of the 20th century relates to how we conceived and designed streets. According to Peter Norton, in his book 'Fighting Traffic', streets did not become places for cars without a protracted, and as he puts it, a bloody and sometimes violent revolution. The result was that city streets which once were the stage set for urban life – where kids played, goods were sold and pedestrians shared the space equally with vehicles – were now seen as largely for vehicle movement, and thus regulations and policies were enacted to enforce a new regime.

32 King Street in Kingston, Jamaica, was built in an era when streets where designed as multifunctional space. Streets like this fully supported the activities of the city and accommodated all users – including pedestrians and non-motorized travel.

33 Constant Spring Road in Kingston, Jamaica, stands in sharp contrast to King Street. It is in a section of the city that was developed circa 1940 and is clearly designed more for cars and less for the comfort of pedestrians.

34 This road in the new town of Portmore, Jamaica, was built in the 1970s, even later than Constant Spring Road and it is even less accommodating of pedestrians. Another important factor of this newer approach to street design is the lack of a coherent relationship between the streets and the buildings. In this new pattern the buildings are set back from the street and do not have a specific orientation to the street, unlike in the older pattern of place making. The changes in design illustrated by these series of pictures is not limited to Jamaica and, in fact, can be considered to be an export from the United States.

31 *"Before the advent of the automobile, the users of city streets were diverse and included children at play and pedestrians at large. By 1930, most streets were primarily motor thoroughfares where pedestrians were condemned as 'jaywalkers.'" Peter Norton argues that to accommodate automobiles, the American city required not only a physical change but also a social one: before the city could be reconstructed for the sake of motorists, its streets had to be socially reconstructed as places where motorists belonged. "It was not an evolution, but a bloody and sometimes violent revolution."*

31

32 Kingston, Jamaica

33 Kingston, Jamaica

34 Portmore, Jamaica

35 The campaigns and battles that led to changes in the design and use of streets was not limited to the Americas. This illustration was created in 1927 and was distributed to school children in the city of Zurich, Switzerland. The goal was to get people to stop using the street as shared space and to promote the idea that streets were for cars and that people should stay on the sidewalk.

36 Prior to World War 2 most city, town and villages in America were laid out with a relatively dense, connected street network, usually in a grid pattern. This example is the street network of Washington, DC, which was unusual in having diagonal streets in addi-tion to the underlying grid pattern. Cities in the post war period expanded by extending the existing grid.

37 The new pattern of development represents a sharp break with the past, as is illustrated in this aerial view of the suburbs of Atlanta, Georgia. All of the factors that we have discussed in this paper are represented here, including the unconnected street network, the large pedestrian-unfriendly arterial streets, and the segregated and fragmented land use pattern. New Urbanism is a response to this pattern of land use which is increasingly being associated with a long list of environmental, social and economic woes.

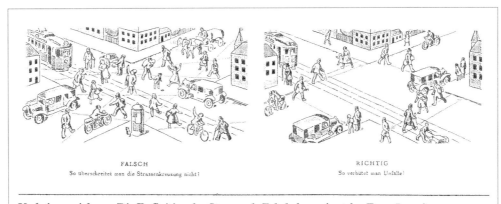

FALSCH
So überschreitet man die Strassenkreuzung nicht!

RICHTIG
So verhütet man Unfälle!

Verkehrserziehung. Die Definition der Strasse als Fahrbahn zwingt den Fussgängerinnen und Fussgängern ein rationalisiertes Verhalten auf. Abbildung aus der *Zürcher Verkehrsfibel*, die 1927 an alle Schulkinder verteilt wurde. (Stadtarchiv Zürich)

35

36

37

38

39

40

38 Some people mistakenly equate New Urbanism to a style of architecture. In practice, New Urbanism is less about the architecture of buildings and much more about the architecture of places. This idea is best expressed in the the Charter of the New Urbanism whose pre-amble states that "*The Congress for the New Urbanism views disinvestment in central cities, the spread of placeless sprawl, increasing separation by race and income, environmental deterioration, loss of agricultural lands and wilderness, and the erosion of society's built heritage as one interrelated community-building challenge.*

We stand for the restoration of existing urban centers and towns within coherent metropolitan regions, the reconfiguration of sprawling suburbs into communities of real neighborhoods and diverse districts, the conservation of natural environments, and the preservation of our built legacy."

The task requires effort to counter and eliminate policies – and also design and financial practices – that are set up to facilitate sprawl as the default approach to place making. This has meant battling against highly entrenched systems that are incredibly hard to counteract. They are found everywhere – from zoning codes, traffic planning and parking polices to insurance and banking regulations.

39 Some successful applications of New Urban principles include the development of new towns like Rosemary Beach in Florida.

40 But New Urbanism has had a marked impact on the revitalization of cities where new urbanist techniques and policies have been successfully used to reverse the trend of suburbanization our cities. This example is from the Logan Circle neighborhood of Washington, DC, which has undergone a remarkable resurgence over the last 10 years. The recently constructed food market in the neighborhood demonstrates many of the principles from the Charter of the New Urbanism for building in an urban neighborhood.

41 New urban principles are also evident in the areas of development in Portland, Oregon, along the Portland streetcar line.

42 New Urbanism in America parallels the movement in Germany and other European countries to build places that do not have the environmental, social and economic drawbacks associated with the contemporary modernist-influenced development pattern that still predominates all over the globe. This example is Vauban, a 1990s extension of the city of Freiburg im Breisgau, Germany. It has many of the design hallmarks of New Urbanism. It also has many features that suggest that, like in the USA, the process of re-learning the craft of place making is still in its early stages of recovering from sprawl making and modernism. Currently, there is not enough synergy between the work being done in Europe and in North America in the effort to develop a 'new' approach to place making. There is a lot that new urbanists could learn from the builders of new towns in Europe, but likewise the new urbanists have perfected approaches and techniques that could enrich the work being done all over Europe in creating more sustainable new towns and cities.

41

42

43

Illustration credits
Norman Garrick

1 *The Triple Threat, Ben Bolgar 2012.*

BEN BOLGAR *Community Capital*

Learning about Sustainability from Historic Settlement

'Sustainability', a rather abused word, is to do with improving the quality of human life while living within the carrying capacity of supporting eco-systems.[1]

Sustainability crystallised as the leading narrative of the environmental movement when Gro Harlem Brundtland was asked in 1983 to chair the World Commission on Environment and Development to address growing concerns with regard to the human and natural environment and the likely impact of that on social and economic development. Brundtland argued that, "the 'environment' is where we live; and 'development' is what we all do in attempting to improve our lot within that abode. The two are inseparable." Hence the focus on sustainable development with the associated definition from the Brundtland report, *Our Common Future*: "Sustainable development is development that meets the needs of the present without compromising the ability of future generations to meet their own needs." Given the egocentric nature of human beings and the desire for self-preservation, a more honest definition of sustainability as defined by Brundtland would be "the perpetuation of human life".

MASTERS OF THE UNIVERSE

Rewind nearly 400 years before that and Galileo, "the father of modern Physics"[2] was busy laying the ground for technological change when he declared that primary qualities were objective and reliable and secondary qualities were subjective and therefore largely unreliable. [3] There began a bifurcation point between the world of subjective mystery, religion and fairy tales to a new world order of the real, the objective, the measurable and the precise, in which the old would be cleared out. This new era of meteoric advances in human achievement accelerating towards the industrial revolution subliminally carried with it the faith in quantity – what could be measured reliably and objectively – over quality – what was subjective and unreliable. Forward again to 2012 and humanity, with all its knowledge and science, is spectacularly failing to turn the oil tanker speeding towards the rocks. The deck chairs have now been turned towards the stern where the aspect is more pleasing and the sun is setting on the horizon.

In terms of the scientific advances that evolved from post-enlightenment thinking few would deny that medicine and particularly anaesthetics have significantly improved the quality of life for billions of people. Indeed, it is now difficult to imagine a world where you can't get access to pretty much every medicine from your local pharmacy and every gadget you need from your phone. Where one used to have a theodolite, metronome, torch, calculator, scanner, computer, camera and telephone all in separate casings of metal, wood and plastic one now has a chic slim-line black or white gadget that even has its own automated secretarial service. What's not to like? But if we can find a moment's peace to pause and reflect on the evidence that climate change, compounded by population increase, not only poses the greatest threat to humanity but is also man-made, we must perhaps ask if qualities, values and common sense should be given more credence than they have been of late in a world where quantifying every last little thing has become the holy grail of human progress.

In 2009 The Prince of Wales delivered the prestigious annual Dimbleby Lecture in London and used the platform to raise awareness of the limits of our own ecosystem and to emphasise that rather than societies being driven solely by financial capital we should see that as a human construct within Natural Capital, a far more real entity:

Back in the 1950's and right up to the 1990's it seemed credible to argue that the human will was the master of creation; that the only acceptable way of thinking was a mechanistic way of thinking; that the Earth's natural resources were just that – resources – to be plundered because they were there for our use, without limit. It was on such terms that we founded our present 'Age of Convenience', a way of living that is now spreading around the world. But for all its achievements, our consumerist society comes at an enormous cost to the Earth and we must face up to the fact that the Earth cannot afford to support it. Just as our banking sector is struggling with its debts – and paradoxically also facing calls for a return to so-called 'old-fashioned', traditional banking – so Nature's life-support systems are failing to cope with the debts we have built up there too. So, if we don't face up to this, then Nature, the biggest bank of all, could go bust. And no amount of quantitative easing will revive it.[4]

One of the difficulties of responding to climate change and carbon reduction targets is that society monitors its success on gross domestic product (GDP), the human construct of production, economic growth and by association consumption. To oversimplify the matter our global economy seems to be largely predicated on growth for growth's sake rather than quality of life and external negative impacts.

THE SCREAM[5]

It is well worth continuing to remind ourselves of what we are facing if the current trends on carbon emissions continue. According to the Intergovernmental Panel on Climate Change, eleven of the twelve hottest years since temperature readings became available occurred between 1995 and 2006. If the global mean temperature cannot be stabilised at less than 2 degrees Celsius then it is likely that temperatures will steadily rise with largely unpredictable but catastrophic results. At 4–5 degrees Celsius warming southern Europe, North Africa and the Middle East will become uninhabitable with people migrating on a mass scale towards the poles. If 5–6 degree warming occurs, the arctic will become ice-free year round, forcing coastal cities to migrate inland. Past 6 degrees the seas become dead zones and 90 per cent of species probably become extinct.[6] [1, 2]

The extraordinary fact is just how rapidly population and consumption have increased in the last century in line with the extraction of cheap oil. One hundred

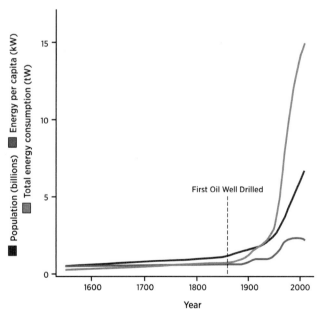

2 Growth of population and energy consumption, adapted from Nature, 2012.

years ago in 1912 the global population stood at only 1.65 billion people meaning it has more than quadrupled since then to over seven billion. Since 1950 we have consumed more natural resources than the total resource consumption prior to that date and since the mid 1960's the demand for resources has doubled. Most of this excessive consumption has occurred in western civilization and so surely the question must be asked: Has the quality of life improved for those citizens in direct relationship to the amount of consumption? In this frenzy of development a few things in society have remained relatively static, for instance the historic cores of the great cities of Paris, London and Rome which silently stand as a reminder of how people lived before we started extending ourselves.

A SLOW AWAKENING

The reality of keeping societies happy and peaceful at a time when we face the triple threat of resource depletion, population increase and climate change is going to be challenging. Already there are signs that governments are seeking measures other than GDP by which to value national achievement. In France, under the last government, Nicholas Sarkozy commissioned Joseph Stiglitz, a leading economist, to explore the possibility of a happiness index as a measure of societal success in addition to GDP, which solely measures economic growth, and which Sarkozy considered no longer sustainable. Importantly, to measure the equality of income, quality of public services and the contentment of citizens in balance with the quality of the environment moves beyond objective measuring of outputs towards a more subtle and subjective set of qualities and outcomes. These softer statistics require polling to ensure accuracy but are equally as valuable to the human condition as quantities. What these indices of happiness suggest is that Western economies are less efficient than others at producing happiness, and that they have become less carbon efficient at producing happiness than they were 40 years ago.[7]

Sarkozy is not alone and in the UK David Cameron has set the Office for National Statistics working on meas-

uring societal well-being as well as economic well-being. The first results were published in July 2012 and even though a cynic might suspect a degree of political 'spin-doctoring', the British public appears remarkably upbeat. The average Briton rates their life satisfaction as 7.4 out of 10, which in one of the worst depressions of the century in economic terms is perhaps surprising. The purpose of the research is explicit in challenging GDP as the sole indicator of a nation's health. Globally the Organisation for Economic Co-operation and Development (OECD) is working on the Better Life Initiative to balance the focus on economics and growth but it is likely to be some time until GDP is knocked off its perch as the meaningful indicator of national success.

However, during this period of cognitive transition we are climbing dangerously to the tipping point of a global warming no-return. There seems to be a sad inevitability that the new enlightened way of behaving which has so improved our quality of life in one dimension will lead to a global nightmare for billions of citizens, through the unintended consequences of man's own clever making.

AND DID THOSE FEET [8]

Given that the pre-war city allowed for a high quality of life with limited consumption of material goods or carbon footprint, it must give us clues as to how human beings went about enhancing their lives with limited resources. In terms of understanding the principles of sustainable development it is sensible to study development that has sustained. At the regional scale settlement patterns of the 1920's, before the acceleration in oil production, showed a balance between humans and the land in terms of food production, trade and settlement. Essentially the network of rural villages for communities working the land, with market towns as regional trading centres and cities as civic hubs, gave us an efficiently scaled set of settlements. The importance of this multiplication of human settlement patterns at various scales is that they demonstrate similar characteristics from one scale to another. In essence one might find an urban village in the middle of London exhibiting very similar physical characteristics to a village in the middle of the countryside. Indeed many villages, which were once rural, now find themselves embedded in the middle of much larger settlements but relatively unchanged physically and still functioning efficiently. Léon Krier, the urban theorist, is someone who for years has championed the concept of polycentric versus monocentric settlement patterns. He compares these settlement patterns to cells found in nature which know their optimal size and then divide into self-similar entities rather than getting bigger and bigger. [3]

The simple notion of a walkable community or 'urban villages' is common to the majority of traditional settlements that out of necessity are scaled around the measure of walking. The practical notion that one would be able to get one's daily needs within 500 metres or a five-minute walk is profound in that it transcends politics and time, creating a simple structuring device for new or existing settlements based on accessibility and walkability. The Prince of Wales's Foundation for Building Community has long been promoting such simple ideals and often starts community planning events by locating walkable neighbourhood catchments on logical primary movement networks and then setting out sensible accessibility indices to help locate various amenities within those neighbourhoods. This applies as much to planning a new community as it does to making existing communities more efficient. [4]

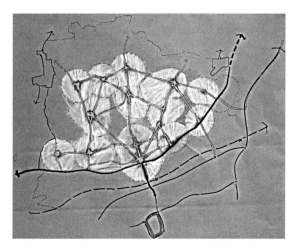

4 Prince's Foundation, catchment structure for Harlow North.

3 Léon Krier, City development, published in The Architectural Tuning of Settlements by Léon Krier.

5 Village of Limington in the Cotswold's.

The movement network upon which settlements and neighbourhoods typically sit can be traced back to a logical route through a particular terrain connecting one place to another. People ideally like to get from one place to another as directly as possible and because we see in straight lines we often walk in them too. However examine historical streets and you will find a deeply subtle series of alignments, with many villages in England having a gentle S-shaped curve to the route containing a straighter section where the high street might be located. [5] Similar routes can be found when people take short-cuts across grassy areas, making their own desire lines which are very rarely straight. In making any new settlement the Foundation believes in the discipline of walking the site many times and trying to trace out by foot where it makes sense for the routes to go. These can be staked out on site and then adjusted as further work to the master plan which is carried out. Each community facility in a plan, such as a shop or school, would act as an attractor of movement and so multiple movement networks should gradually be traced over the plan to simulate the real movements that are likely to occur in the place over time.

Clearly infrastructure related to trains, cars and bicycles is important also, particularly at the national and regional scale, but the most enduring and useful principle is still one of walkability. The beauty of walking is that it reduces energy consumption, carbon emissions and pollution as well as keeping people fitter and more sociable. With a serious epidemic of obesity [9] and the fragmentation of community[10], walking as a way of getting about locally is sensible on almost every level.

MY ROCK OF AGES[11]

When one looks at the physical growth of UK market towns, such as Northampton, in more detail one can see the formation of a civic square, a market square and a series of radiating streets leading north, east, south and west. [6] One can also see perhaps the most fundamental attribute of the historical city, the idea of buildings making streets that define public and pri-

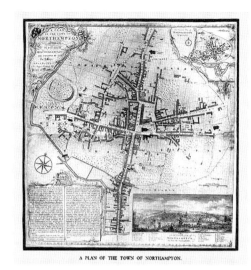

6 Northampton, Town plan, 1749.

vate spaces, with public to the front and private to the back. Simply put, by lining buildings up so that collectively they create public space through which people can move and meet is a fundamental part of any civilization. The post-war settlement pattern of zoned development that separated the components of a town or city is not only inefficient in terms of the amount of infrastructure it gives over to the car but is also anti-social in that it doesn't create any public realm to speak of. Given that the very basis of civilization is based on people agreeing to live together for greater ends in coherent settlement patterns, the deconstruction and fragmentation of the social glue of the street is inherently unsustainable.

What we also learn from the traditional city is some notion of sequencing or phasing growth. It is true that most historical places grew quite slowly compared to the speed with which we now make new places. That said, it is perhaps a mistake to link organic growth to unplanned growth as whilst there may be less documentation about the formal planning of places in the past people didn't have the same means or needs to spend time recording their proposed actions on paper. Things tended to be more direct and most of the human resource put into preparing the ground and building rather than lengthy legislation, master plans, com-

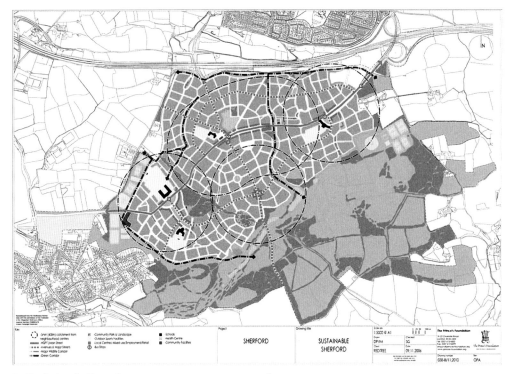

7 *Sherford walkable catchment structure on movement network.*

plex contracts, planning applications or costly legal challenges.

When Christopher Alexander, author of *A Pattern Language: Towns, Buildings, Construction* was receiving the Congress for the New Urbanism's prestigious Athena Medal he made a specific point about the difference between understanding the product of development and the process involved. He lauded the fact that New Urbanists bothered to study, replicate and modify historical settlement patterns but warned against copying the physical product of traditional architecture and urbanism without fully understanding the process that had given rise to it. He suggested that if one copied the form alone, one could still end up with a soulless product if the design and building process itself was lifeless. Whilst this is a fundamental point, what is difficult to grasp in today's context is how such simple building processes and practices in the past, with limited resources and means, gave rise to such beautiful and sustainable places of a quality

we can only dream of today. Therein lies the Holy Grail – how did our ancestors around the world make sustainable town-building look so easy?

With specific reference to Europe the most relevant answers to today's dilemma may well be found in the 17th to 19th century development of cities whether in Paris, London or Berlin. This period, generally speaking, saw the overlaying of a more regular or repetitive form of development over a more subtle and organic series of movement networks. The older networks themselves would most probably have paid quite a bit of attention to the land in terms of geology and topography with the newer networks seeking to regularise the city either for the purposes of security, efficiency or grandeur. It is in this interplay between the more organic and the planned that perhaps the right balance can be struck both in terms of efficiency as sustainability. The relentless grid, for instance may be as efficient in terms of land-use but in terms of livability, contrast and intensity falls short. Likewise a plan without structure or formality can lack both the efficiency and beauty of some forms of human organisation. By studying traditional settlement patterns that have sustained we can learn from both the similarity and differences. The elements that are universal across the world give us the main armatures for human settlement whereas the components that change based on culture, materials and climate give us the language by which we can develop sustainable places and upgrade traditional elements to meet new challenges.

In the Prince's Foundation's urban plan at Sherford these principles of walkable neighbourhoods, logical street networks and urban blocks defining public and private realm can be seen. [7] Although the plan is for a completely new place, it seeks to incorporate the attributes of a place that has developed over time in a logical and legible way. The epicentre of the town is the main cross-roads where the town centre is located with three main walkable neighbourhoods on primary arterial routes, all with primary schools and a shop at their centre. The main physical structuring device was based on the notion of accessibility to services based on walkable distances.

The rule of thumb of daily needs being accessible within a five-minute walk is a useful starting point, but it is important to calibrate any community for all of the amenities in that place based on a series of factors including frequency of use, space, catchment and to whom the amenity is catering. For instance small children's play areas would occur more frequently and be more accessible than multi-use games areas or parks. The following diagram shows the accessibility indices for Sherford arrived through both debate and observation. [8]

ABSORBING TECHNOLOGY

Sustainable urban and built physical fabric is always likely to outlast fast moving technologies or trends. The following diagram was developed by the Prince's Foundation in order to understand the layering of settlements over time in relation to how quickly attributes were likely to change. [9] Slowly changing attributes like hills or rivers (Nature) are at the bottom

whilst fast changing attributes like fashion are towards the top. On the right are the human responses to such attributes; so with Nature we might *steward* those elements and with quick changing fashion we might *absorb* it into the fabric. The important point to

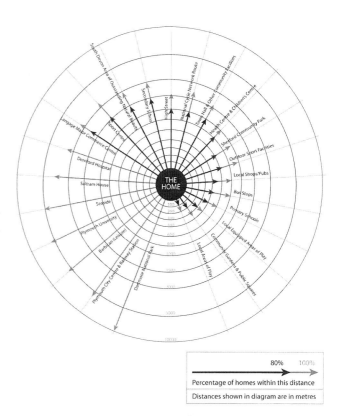

8 Accessibility indices developed for Sherford.

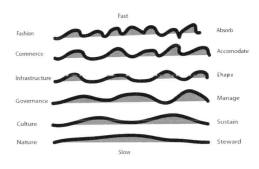

Rates of Change in Cities and Towns

9 Prince's Foundation, "rates of change" diagram, after Robert Brandt.

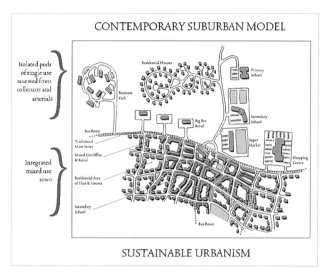

*10 Prince's Foundation, "sustainable vs. unsustainable urbanism"
diagram.*

make about complex systems such as settlement patterns, is to make sure that new technologies or trends
which might only be similar for a short period of time
do not disrupt elements of infrastructure that are on
slower frequencies. Therefore, if the current trend in
retail is for big boxes storing large amounts of goods,
they should not disrupt pedestrian infrastructure that
might in the long term be more sustainable.

Another example of a new technology that has had
perhaps the biggest impact on traditional settlement
patterns is the motor car. [10] Not only has it allowed
the proliferation of the sprawling suburban layout but
it has turned pedestrian thoroughfares into traffic
routes with noise, pollution and safety issues for

11 Sherford High Street, Watercolour by Chris Draper.

residents. It is safe to assume that a town will long
outlast current car design and the move towards
cleaner and quieter vehicles may make a difference to
how we design our streets, but for now our assumption has been to incorporate vehicles in a way that
strikes a balance between public, transport, private
transport, bicycles and pedestrians. The busier streets
need a cross-sectional proportion that is generous
enough to mitigate noise and pollution and the secondary and tertiary street need design so that traffic
speeds are slowed and pedestrians are given equal
priority over the car.

The most intense and demanding design challenge in
Sherford was the high street itself as it is both the
place of maximum through movement and also the
main heart of the community needing to provide the
setting for dynamic social cohesion. Again learning
from historic settlement we sought out the most successful traditional place that seemed to have ab-
sorbed large numbers of vehicles but functioned well
and was a pleasant place to be. This was Marlbor-
ough in Wiltshire, where the broad high street affec-
tively acts as a linear square. The two main lanes are
bordered by short-term parallel parking on the left,
long-term diagonal parking in the middle and parking
for the larger stores behind the building frontages
within the urban block. In Sherford this basic layout
has been refined to meet modern standards, allow for
a priority bus route and also allow for the future incor-
poration of a tram system in the central parking area
should it be required. [11]

Exactly the same thinking was applied simultaneously
during the design with the green infrastructure with
the main water courses and landscape features
threading their way through the plan in an interconnected way. The collision between man-made and
natural systems through the plan gives a richness and
quality to any place where the idea of town and country interface directly. The main challenge with urban
and natural form is to get the quantity and type correct as too much open space with limited ecological
or recreational value could destroy the urban coher-
ence and density needed to make the local amenities
perform properly. [12]

An example of this at an urban scale in one of the Prince's Foundation's projects at Upton is where a sustainable urban drainage system is incorporated into the streetscape. [13] One street is more formal in its architecture and planting while the other provides a horse trail and in time will appear more natural. The mews street that cuts through the block collects water underground and all hold back water to avoid flooding. This is just one example of how traditional forms of settlement pattern have been used and adapted to absorb a new method of dealing with water run-off.

Another example of upgrading tradition is the Prince's Natural House constructed at the Building Research Establishment's Innovation Park. [14] This takes as its precedent the English paired villa, a particular type of dwelling largely built in the 18th century and inspired by John Nash. This simple form of dwelling paired two houses together to imply one larger house making the streetscape feel less urban and giving greater value to the dwelling. These houses are typically wider in plan than the flat fronted terraces being built at the same time and are better suited to adaptation into multiple dwellings. The Natural House is built of natural materials that have been upgraded to make them better performing with the brick walls being replaced by aerated clay block for better insulation and improved building speed. The chimney stack of the older house has changed and in the Natural House the smoke is separated from the air with two flues extracting smoke from energy-efficient wood burners and the two other flues housing a self-regulating passive air ventilation system.

NOTHING IS PERMANENT EXCEPT CHANGE

From the scale of the region, the town, the neighbourhood, the block, the plot and finally building, change is inevitable. So when designing a town that might take 30 years to build and needs to survive for thousands of years how can we make sure that we lay down a pattern that doesn't compromise the ability of future generations to meet their own needs? One of the most complex but necessary components for this

12 Green infrastructure and sustainable urban drainage at Sherford, computer image by Architecture in Motion.

13 Sustainable urban drainage in Upton, Northampton.

14 The Prince's Natural House at the Building Research Establishment's Innovation Park.

in a town plan is the land-use plan. Returning to Sherford this component of the design was one of the most hotly debated and enlightening. To understand what quantum of non-residential activities one might associate with a town of 16,000 people we sought the help of Savills research arm. They decided that the most accurate exercise would be to find similarly located and scaled towns and count the activities found

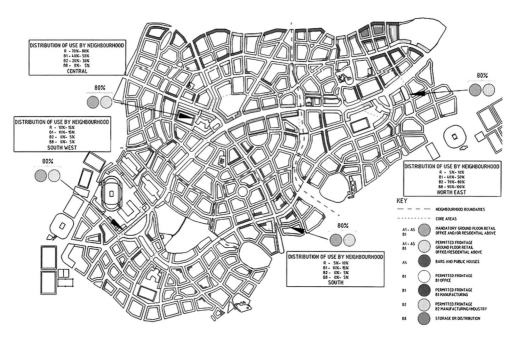

15 Sherford land-use plan.

in the historic place. The diversity and quantity of uses were astounding and clearly showed how traditional urban and architectural fabric is highly adaptable, absorbing non-residential uses over time. The locations of uses in a traditional town are finely integrated and have serious implications for what building type one chooses to locate in a particular location. Because of the implied economy of movement, as a rule of thumb, the buildings needing to absorb the highest frequency of change are on the primary networks where retail, office and even light industrial are best located. To allow for maximum flexibility over time the land-use plan at Sherford is defined by frontages and also takes account of uses above ground floor. By creating a system of allocating a percentage of frontages to an area, future flexibility is built in both during construction and also in terms of permitted development once the town is built. There is a clear correlation between mix of uses and the movement network. [15]

As part of the process for designing Sherford a Sustainability Framework was developed to inform the work. It became hard to simplify the sections and so the final list consisted of:

– community involvement and governance
– connectivity – local to global
– local centres – organic growth
– neighbourhood structure – the high street
– evidence of the land – landscape
– ecological and historical patterns
– settling into the land – build form responding to landscape
– pedestrian movement
– the logic of the block
– urban grain – block types
– land uses – accessibility to local amenities
– employment and businesses – opportunities and placement
– local economy – recycling, equity and food
– housing – balance and range
– transport – mobility access and parking
– public realm – street types
– massing – legibility and daylight
– density

– creating appropriate urbanity
– infrastructure – utilities
– energy – conservation and renewables
– waste
– environment – minimizing pollution
– adaptability – building types and lifespan
– local resources – minimising movement
– cultural heritage – protecting existing and creating local identity

During the lengthy design process the Building Research Establishment were also engaged to audit the elements and developed the notion of the GreenPrint, a tool later developed in full to assess the sustainability of new developments. The seven headings listed below cover a range of issues and go into considerable detail, breaking down each of the sections into component parts and giving it a score. [16]

The ability to reflect on the Prince's Foundation's own sustainability framework and compare it to another framework developed by the Country's leading light on sustainability, the Building Research Establishment, was extremely valuable. The biggest issue that arose was the degree to which almost all of the issues were connected in some way and so assessing an issue in isolation and giving it a score was potentially meaningless without looking at its relationship to the whole or other related issues. This raised two main problems: the fact that each issue in sustainable development has become a specialism, with its own focus and language; and that those particular issues were quantified and weighted without being related to the whole. The desire to explain how something could be sustainable and the ability to audit it were potentially destroying the very thing that makes something more sustainable in the first place.

INVISIBLE THREAD

In response to this work and other projects the Prince's Foundation embarked on a journey to try to look for another way of approaching sustainability. For this a number of sustainability frameworks were analysed and the inherent problems of quantifying and separateness discussed. After many months of messy discourse the basis of an idea began to emerge. The main idea was how to describe things to which it makes sense to add a quantity of some kind, the overlay was how to add value to that context and the other overarching element was more to do with a process by which things had a chance of becoming more or less sustainable as a structure.

Returning to Christopher Alexander and his work the *Nature of Order*, there is a section in the first book where he describes life like a Persian carpet – a series of patterns, or centres, which are in fact self-supporting. There are many self-similar patterns found at different scales with some similar and others different. What makes the pattern strong is that the patterns are mutually supportive of the whole. We began to think of a sustainability framework being more similar to a weave where the vertical threads might be the more usual attributes of sustainability – namely Social, Natural and Financial Capital with Built Capital added to represent the physical framework. The cross-weave we decided should be a series of values more similar in nature to qualities that gave meaning to the capitals themselves and began to stitch them together – namely Rooted, Connected, Balanced, Resilient and Prudent. [17] The process of design is to record both positive and negative attributes for the entire framework and then begin to develop strategies that build on the positive attributes and transform the negatives. The most sustainable action or strategy is the one that has the most positive and transformative impact on the different areas

Overall Performance Rating: Exemplar

Figure 1: Sustainability Framework Summary

16 Building Research Establishment's sustainability assessment, Sherford.

17 Prince's Foundation, community capital framework.

of the framework. In this way strategies are seen as mutually supportive patterns that weave together through different parts of the framework. The activities are as much to do with the value judgments that are taken by communities in relation to issues than by specialists in relation to quantifying assets – in fact the two are considered simultaneously.

Key to implementing the Community Capital Framework is the Prince's Foundation's "Enquiry by Design" process which engages the local community and key stakeholders in any design process. The process involves four key steps of listening, examining, diagnosing and creating solutions and strategies. Specialists work together with community representatives in parallel multi-disciplinary groups when developing design hypotheses. These hypotheses are presented and the commonalities drawn-out, discussed and recorded. The emerging consensus developed in terms of consolidation plans or documents which are then critiqued by specialists at the appropriate time and refined. This process is referred to as 'cross-cutting', where groups oscillate between being holistic to specialist. It is this process that allows the weaving of attributes with qualities and also draws out the best of local intelligence and emotion.

REDISCOVERING VALUES

In 1972 Gregory Bateson, the English anthropologist and cyberneticist, published his book *Steps to an Ecology of Mind* in which he warns of the state of scientific hubris, where man becomes locked into a state of narrowed perception based on false knowledge. He talks of the problems of man attempting to control the whole of cybernetics with linear systems based on his own rules when the real cybernetic system operates in a non-linear fashion outside those intellectual constructs. Bateson suggests that scientific humility is required, rather than the inherent arrogance which has the potential to damage and destroy the supreme cybernetic system. This is not dissimilar to the Prince of Wales's view that the exciting developments of the Enlightenment gave birth to a cognitive shift in western society where man started to see himself as outside nature and that nature was there to be exploited for the good of man. The Prince constantly speaks of the importance of man learning to see himself as 'part of nature', rather than 'apart from nature' to awaken a concern for earth's ecosystem or natural capital.

Half a century on from Bateson's warning we find ourselves in a position where the ecological damage is real and far from being able to change to an 'ecology of mind'; we are locked into patterns of living fuelled by economic development, consumption and more and more statistics and measures to tell us what we are doing wrong. In all probability, and with robust statistics at our fingertips, we are possibly at the point of no return and should focus on minimising our impact on ecological systems and on the adaptation of our patterns of living. Key to facing up to the challenge ahead is recognising that community is the social glue of civilization and that keeping societies connected and strong in times of fundamental change is critical. If we start to look towards building community capital then this is perhaps the most sustainable and complete task for the future of people and their relationship with each other and the planet. The word community has two current meanings: the first has to do with a group of interacting people living in some proximity or relationship and the second is a biological term, describing a group of interacting living organisms sharing a populated environment. If we see ourselves as within nature, then perhaps the second definition is all that is needed. As The Prince of Wales put it in his Dimbleby Lecture in 2009:

Facing the future, therefore, requires a shift from a reductive, mechanistic approach to one that is more balanced and integrated with nature's complexity – one that recognises not just the build-up of financial capital, but the equal importance of what we already have – environmental capital and, crucially, what I might best call 'community capital'. That is, the networks of people and organisations, the post offices and pubs, the churches and village halls, the mosques, temples and bazaars – the wealth that holds our communities together; that enriches people's lives through mutual support, love, loyalty and identity. Just as we have no way of accounting for the loss of the natural world, contemporary economics has no way of accounting for the loss of this community capital.[13]

HARMONY

Key to the Prince's Foundation's work is the idea of Harmony. This has had many meanings throughout history, perhaps most fully developed is the theory of music where sounds are made pleasant to the ear. It is effectively about how things fit together in a pleasing way or about compatible relationships of parts to wholes. Harmony must therefore be a shared act of relationships in an ever changing environment. In order to be able to understand harmony, one must pay as much attention to the relationships between things as to the things themselves. If one accepts that the city is the most powerful physical representation of a society's ideas and beliefs then it is surely the relationships between the buildings that give it harmony. The shared relationships of communities within the historical city are evident in the shared spaces such as streets and squares where public life is played out. The destruction of the street, so apparent in post-war planning, could yet be seen as a metaphor for the lack of understanding of relationships in a community and the true nature of the sustainability of living systems.

A civilization remains healthy and strong as long as it contains in its centre some creative ideal that binds in its members in a rhythm of relationship. It is a relationship [and this is most important] which is beautiful and not merely utilitarian.[14]

The Prince of Wales

Illustration credits
Figs. 1–5, 7–17: The Prince's Foundation
Fig. 6: City Planning Archives Northampton

Footnotes
1 International Union for Conservation of Nature and Natural Resources/United Nations Environment Programme/WWF-World Wide Fund For Nature,1991.
2 Manfred Weidhorn, *The Person of the Millennium. The Unique Impact of Galileo on World History*, New York, Lincoln, Shanghai 2005, p. 155.
3 From: Brian Goodwin, "Reclaiming a Life of Quality", in: *The Journal of Consciousness Studies*, vol. 6, nos. 11–12, 1999, pp. 229–35.
4 The Richard Dimbleby Lecture, titled "Facing the Future" as delivered by HRH The Prince of Wales, St James's Palace State Apartments, London 8th July 2009.
5 "I sensed a scream passing through nature", diary entry Edward Munch 1892 giving rise to *The Scream*.
6 Mark Lynas, *Six Degrees. Our Future on a Hotter Planet*, London 2007.
7 New Economics Foundation, "The Happy Planet Index", 2009, available: http://www.neweconomics.org/publications/happy-planet-index-20 (visited August 2012)
8 "And did those feet in ancient times", poem by William Blake c. 1808.
9 Statistics on obesity, physical activity and diet: England 2012, NHS.
10 Changing UK report, University of Sheffield, December 2008.
11 *Rock of Ages*, Christian hymn by Reverend Augustus Montague Toplady written in 1763.
12 Quote attributed to Heraclitus, 535-475 BC, in: *Lives of the Philosophers* by Diogenes Laertius.
13 The Richard Dimbleby Lecture, titled "Facing the Future" as delivered by HRH The Prince of Wales, St James's Palace State Apartments, London 8th July 2009.
14 A speech by The Prince of Wales at the unveiling of the bust of Tagore, 11th July 2011.

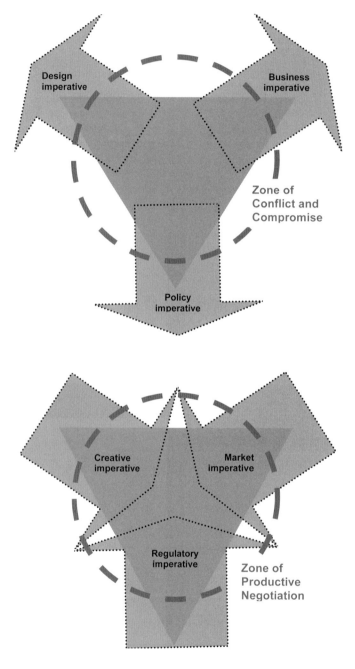

Design
imperative

Business
imperative

Zone of
Conflict and
Compromise

Policy
imperative

Creative
imperative

Market
imperative

Regulatory
imperative

Zone of
Productive
Negotiation

1 Zones of conflict and compromise and of productive negotiation

MATTHEW CARMONA *Design Coding*

Mediating the Tyrannies of Practice

In England until the mid-1990s, design quality was either given lip service to, or actively excluded from the political agenda, resulting in open inter-professional conflict, sub-standard design outcomes, and the resort of the public sector to crude development standards as a substitute for design. In this lecture, it is argued that at the root of these problems were three tyrannies of practice that actively undermined positive engagement in design. More recently, driven by local and national growth agendas, public administrations have increasingly sought policy instruments to once again engage in the delivery of design quality, one of these being design coding. This lecture uses the example of design codes to explore the process-based tyrannies, and the potential of such tools to overcome them.

This lecture is segmented into four main parts. It starts by presenting three tyrannies through the literature, concluding in the process that the typical large-scale development project is hampered by its journey from inception to realisation occurring within a context of professional conflict and compromise. The second part discusses the role of design coding, exploring how site-specific coding differs from generic development standards. Drawing on an empirical research study, the third part explores the use and potential of design codes and their value in helping to mediate the tyrannies of practice. A final part draws conclusions.

1. THE THREE TYRANNIES

The built environment is a collective endeavour, influenced by a diversity of stakeholders, each with a role to play in shaping what we see and experience as the architecture, urban form, public space and infrastructure that constitutes the urban environment. In her 'Powergram', McGlynn argues that developers have the real power to shape the built environment through their ability to fund development. The state has power over some aspects of design through their regulatory powers (particularly through the planning processes), while designers have wide ranging responsibility but little real power. Instead, they gain their influence through their unique professional skill (to design) and via their professional and technical knowledge. The community has almost no power, or only indirectly through the right to complain to those with regulatory authority, whom (usually) they elect.

Taking these ideas further, Bentley (1999) postulates four potential relationships between the designer and the developer: *Heroic Form-Giver; Master-and-Servant; Market Signals, and The Battlefield.* Bentley argues that the latter is the most common scenario, and reflects the fact that different actors bring different professional expertise to the table, while the resulting development is shaped by how these actors negotiate with each other to achieve their objectives.

Individual development episodes are likely to adopt different relationships or even different combinations of the relationships, depending on the relative power positions of stakeholders in each case. Moreover, the field is much more complex, as discussed above, with many competing stakeholder influences determining the final form of the built environment; the battlefield is in fact multi-actor, multi-objective and multi-dimensional. Nevertheless, Bentley's metaphors, the idea of conflicting and varied power relationships, and the notion of multiple stakeholder aspirations, can each be understood in terms of the modes of praxis from which they emerge.

These can be considered in terms of three distinct traditions – creative, market-driven, and regulatory – each with a major impact on the built environment as eventually experienced. At their worst, each can be characterised as a particular form of professional 'tyranny', with the potential to impact negatively on the design quality of development proposals. The word tyranny is favoured here because it epitomises a single-minded pursuit of narrow ends in a manner that undermines, or oppresses, the aspirations of others. Though actual practice is not typically situated at such extremes, there is value in exploring these positions which are extensively discussed in the literature and which, it is contended, to greater or lesser degrees underpin all practice.

The creative tyranny

The first tyranny results from the fetishizing of design where the image, rather than the inherent value – economic, social or environmental – is of paramount concern, and where the freedom to pursue the creative process is valued above all else. Such agendas are most closely associated with the architectural profession, often under a guise of rejecting what is sometimes seen as a further tyranny, that of 'context'. Perpetuated by the dominant model of architectural education, and by the continuing impact of Modernism (Walters 2007: 96), many designers see all forms of regulation as limiting their freedom for self-expression: "It is time to challenge the tawdry and compromised architecture. […] Instead we must seek a new sensibility […] one that refuses to bow to preservation, regulation and mediation." (Mantownhuman 2008: 3) In this mode of praxis, the aspiration is for "discovery, experimentation, innovation".

Lang (2005: 384–385) questions the importance of creativity. For him, the design professions place great esteem on what they see as 'creative' designers; those individuals or companies are able to challenge the status quo by producing schemes that depart from the norm in response to a perceived problem in the name of art, or simply to further careers: "Those observers who regard urban design as a fine art would argue for little or no outside interference into what an individual designer/artist does. The population simply has to live with the consequences in the name of Art." Analysing fifty international urban design projects of the last 50 years, he argues that this 'art defence' has often been used to justify design decisions that have later proved detrimental to the enjoyment of the city. To him, this is simply antisocial – a conclusion also reached through a body of Joseph Rowntree Foundation-funded research in the UK which found that in focusing on the aesthetic qualities of public spaces, designers often ignored more fundamental factors about how those spaces will actually be used as social places (Worpole & Knox 2007: 13).

The market tyranny

The second tyranny reflects the argument that the market knows best, and what sells counts. In the UK, this argument has most frequently and most vociferously been made in relation to the speculative housing market, where house builders have long campaigned to be given a free hand to use their standard housing designs and layouts on the basis that they know their market (Carmona 2001: 105–109). Design quality is here "perceived by developers as a complex mix of factors which include dominant economic aspects of supply and demand revolving around costs and sales potential – buildability, standardisation, market assessment, customer feedback – within which the visual or spatial quality is a secondary set of values." (Heriot-Watt University 2007: 2)

In this market, architects have often been excluded altogether from the development process, while because producers are primarily concerned with their profitability and have typically (pre-credit crunch) built in a speculative market where demand exceeds supply, they have been willing and able to produce the lowest quality development that will sell and gain the necessary permissions without too much delay. As Rowley (1998: 172) has argued, they build 'appropriate' rather than 'sustainable' quality.

Lang (2005: 381) asks "Who leads?", concluding that in capitalist countries, private corporations are the drivers of urban development; while Welling's (2006) instructive analysis of the British house building industry reveals that within these corporations it has been personal ambition, stock market position and market share that has driven their agendas. Thus issues such as design quality or sustainability are simply part of the context that needs to be negotiated: (I) when it is in the interest of the corporation to do so, for example if it returns higher profits (Carmona *et al* 2001); (II) when relevant permissions (in the UK: critically planning permission, highways adoption and building regulations) are dependant on it (Heriot-Watt University 2007: 3); (III) when the particular site context requires it (for example complex brownfield sites). (Tiesdell & Adams 2004: 25)

The regulatory tyranny

For some, the regulatory tyranny can be analysed (and challenged) in terms of the political economy it represents – as an attempt to correct market failure. Van Doren (2005: 45; 64), for example, argues that regulation is inherently costly and inefficient, but difficult to change because of political support for it from 'Bootleggers' (special interests who gain economically from the existence of regulation) and 'Baptists' (those who do not like the behaviour of others and want government to restrict it). He cites the work of regulatory economists who have generally come out against regulation, arguing that in most cases no market failure existed in the first place. So, while admitting that design regulation has not been subject to such analysis, he concludes it will inevitably create barriers to change and innovation.

Encapsulating these positions and, in the process, distorting the workings of a 'natural' market might be the reactionary local politician proclaiming 'we know what we like and we like what we know', or the unbending municipal technocrat determined that 'rules is rules'. The tyranny also reflects McGlynn's (1994) concern that the state only has real power through the right to say "no" to development proposals via the series of overlapping regulatory regimes – planning, building control, conservation, highways adoption, environmental protection, etc. – but that the power to make positive proposals is limited by it typically being the private sector that has access to resources; both financial (to deliver development) and skills (to design it).

Regulatory processes themselves reflect one of two major types: either they are based on fixed legal frameworks with unquestioning administrative decision-making, or they are discretionary, where a distinction is drawn between law and policy; the latter enacted through 'guiding' plans, skilled professional interpretation in the light of local circumstances, and political decision-making (Reade 1987: 11). Typically most regulatory regimes represent a mix of the two. In the UK, for example, planning, conservation and environmental protection are discretionary (although a shortage of key skills among the professionals charged with their interpretation can lead authorities back in the direction of adopting fixed standards). (Carmona 2001: 225–227) Building control and highways adoption, by contrast, are fixed technical processes, not open to interpretation or appeal.

Both forms of decision-making (reflecting the local politician/council technocrat positions above) contribute to the tyranny: the first because of its perceived arbitrary, inconsistent and subjective nature; the second because of its lack of flexibility or inability to consider non-standard approaches (Booth in Cullingworth 1999: 43). Moreover, the diversity of regulatory processes and systems, and their often disjointed, uncoordinated and even contradictory nature, adds to a perception that "[…] a marathon of red tape needs to be run." (Imrie & Street 2006: 7)

A zone of conflict and compromise

The tyrannies represent extremes, perhaps even caricatures, but arguably they also reflect realities that practitioners from whichever side of the tyranny trinity are repeatedly faced with during the development process. They result from profoundly different motivations, respectively: peer approval, profit, a narrowly defined view of public interest, very different modes of working and associated professional knowledge fields, respectively: design, management/finance, and social/technical expertise. Long driving practice and debate both in the UK (Carmona 1998) and US (Ellis 2002: 262), often resulted in perpetuated profound and ingrained stakeholder conflicts within the development process (see Carmona *et al* 2003) and led to sub-standard development solutions based on conflict, compromise and delay (CABE 2007a).

At the heart of each is also a different and overriding imperative, respectively to achieve an innovative design solution (within given constraints of site, budget, brief, etc.), to make a good return on investment (in order to sustain a viable business), and to satisfy a broad range of public policy objectives. As these are often in opposition to each other, the result will be a three way tug of war, with the central ground stretched thinly within what can be characterised as a zone of conflict and compromise. [1]

2. FROM DEVELOPMENT STANDARDS TO DESIGN CODES

This caricature has long typified development processes in the UK (Bateman 1995) and the US (Duany *et al* 2000: 109; 180), particularly in the residential sector. Thus while attention and resources have tended to be focussed on urban centres, rather than in predominantly residential areas (Colomb 2007), it is in the latter areas where the standard of design is open to greatest criticism (when judged by the satisfaction of new residents with their neighbourhoods — CABE 2007b) and to greatest challenge (when judged by the complaints of existing communities faced with the prospect of new development in their backyard — Savage 2001). The need to deliver large new housing allocations while avoiding the revolt of suburban and rural England, led the UK Government to review the potential of design coding to deliver better design and a smoother regulatory process.

In February 2003, the Government launched its Sustainable Communities Plan for England, setting out its long-term ambition to create sustainable communities in urban and rural areas to meet the increasing demand for new homes, particularly in the South East (ODPM 2003). An implicit assumption in this and other related policy documents was that to achieve the government's challenging targets for housing, new delivery mechanisms were needed. Following the launch of the Sustainable Communities Plan, there was growing media debate about the potential use of design codes as a mechanism to deliver the large-scale housing development envisaged by the plan, spurred on by high-profile visits made by the then Deputy Prime Minister — John Prescott — to codes-based New Urbanist schemes in the USA, most notably Seaside in Florida. Coding of one form or another is nothing new. Different forms of regulation of the built environment have occurred throughout recorded history (Gardiner 2004: 28; Southworth & Ben Joseph 2003; Rowland & Howe 1999; Carmona *et al* 2006b). Many of the development standards currently used to guide the design of build-ings and the urban environment can be described as coding, of sorts, controlling almost every aspect of the built environment:

- National building regulations are a set of codes that dictate the internal and (to some degree) the external design of buildings
- Highway standards (national and local) control a good part of the public realm through their impact on road and footpath design and layout (often dis-astrously)
- Planning standards (national and local) dictate density levels, space between buildings, parking requirements, open space requirements, and so forth
- Secured by design criteria determine lines of sight, permeability, access points, etc.
- Emergency service access guidelines dictate dis-tances between buildings and points of access
- Health and safety standards are increasingly per-vasive across the built environment

Ben-Joseph (2005) traces the evolution of the 'hidden codes' that dictate much of the form and function of urban space around the world. He argues that the original purpose and value of these regulations are often forgotten as bureaucracies implement the stand-ards with little regard to their actual rationale, and even less to their knock-on effects. Furthermore, most of these are limited in their scope and technical in their aspirations and are neither generated from a physical vision of the intended place nor any understanding of a particular site or context (DCLG 2006a: 11).

Instead, these forms of development standards are about achieving minimum requirements across the board (regardless of site context) and in many cases the slavish adherence to such standards has led to the creation of bland and unattractive places (HBF & RIBA 1990; Cullen 1961: 133–137). Arguably this represents a classic case of regulatory (rather than market) fail-ure. Indeed Ben-Joseph (2005: XXI) has observed that today we excel at making development standards but

frequently fail to make good places. In doing so he makes a cogent argument for the existence of the regulatory tyranny.

A site-specific tool

To what extent can the use of design codes as a policy instrument overcome or mediate between the conflict-ing tyrannies? The evidence on the ground suggests that coding in the form of generic (i.e. non site-specif-ic) development standards is unlikely to assist the delivery of better places. Moreover, faced with a per-ceived increase in regulation of different types, archi-tects (Imrie & Street 2006) and developers (Heriot-Watt University 2007: 3) have become increasingly concerned about the impact this has on their room to manoeuvre – their 'opportunity space' – or their space to deliver, respectively, creative and profitable solu-tions. The key question, therefore, is what is a good code and whether such a tool can be used to deliver public interest objectives such as more housing and better places, while still allowing for creative archi-tectural design and enhanced economic value (the preoccupations of the other two components in the tyranny trinity)?

As used in England, the term 'design code' refers to a distinct form of detailed design guidance that stipu-lates the three dimensional components of a particu-lar development without establishing the overall de-sign vision or outcomes (see CABE 2004a, reported in full in Carmona *et al* 2006b). Design codes were seen as providing clarity over what constitutes acceptable design quality for a particular site or area, thereby (in principle at least) achieving a level of certainty for developers and the local community, and, within an appropriate planning framework, helping to improve the speed of delivery (ODPM 2005: 5). Used in this way, and unlike generic development standards, they provide a positive statement about the desired quali-ties of a particular place.

As such, design codes are site-specific tools, typically building upon the design vision contained in a master plan, development framework or other site- or area-based visions. The codes themselves focus on urban design principles aimed at delivering better quality places, for example the requirements for streets, blocks, massing and so forth, but may also cover landscape, architectural and building performance issues such as those aiming to increase energy efficiency. They encompass what in New Urbanist parlance has come to be known as form-based codes (Burdette 2004).

A national pilot programme

For Ministers in England, design codes seemed to hold the promise of a new and different approach and in 2005 they funded a national pilot programme to fully test the potential of design coding. A research programme, led by the present author, evaluated nineteen case studies of three types:

– Seven 'pilot' projects at the start of the design/development process where design codes were to be produced as an integral part of evolving development projects. The development of these codes was monitored from their early stages.
– A retrospective evaluation of eight 'advanced' coded projects, where codes had already been pre-pared and used independently of the pilot programme. In these case studies, development had already been delivered on the ground using design codes.
– Four 'non-code' projects which used other forms of detailed design guidance. These examples were chosen as comparisons, and were also advanced in the sense that they had all been used on-site to deliver projects in various stages of completion.

The case studies reflected a geographical spread, a range of different development and physical contexts, as well as variety in size, ownership and stakeholder engagement. The monitoring and evaluation process was structured using a common method for all of the case studies, with case studies analysed in terms of their approach to each stage of a hypothetical coding process from code inception to build out. [2] See DCLG 2006c for a detailed discussion of methodology, case studies and findings.

Initial stakeholder reactions – the critiques

The announcement of the national pilot programme brought immediate and negative reaction in the professional press, particularly in specialist architectural trade journals. The reaction was further stoked by the

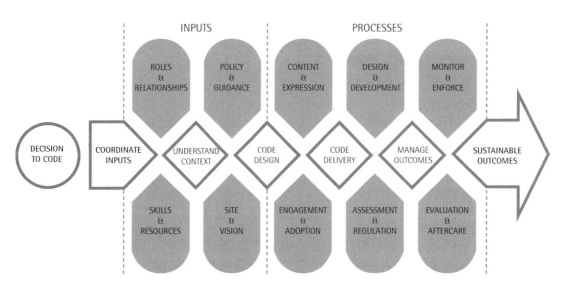

2 A hypothetical coding process

Deputy Prime Minister's visit to Seaside – the film set for the film the *Truman Show* (1998) in which an insurance salesman discovers his entire life is actually a TV show. The nightmarish vision – at least in some commentators' minds – was of waves of *Truman Show*-like dystopia inexorably spreading across England.

Alongside the more predictable headlines, a range or reoccurring critiques appeared across the press arguing that design codes posed a significant danger on a number of counts. These directly attacked what the writers saw as an attempt to extend the tyranny of regulation through the introduction of design coding. In making the arguments, however, they directly reflected creative and market tyranny perspectives.

One set of critiques focussed on design outcomes, suggesting that design codes would:

A. Suffocate the creativity of designers by reducing their scope to innovate
B. Deliver only traditional design solutions through an in-built presumption against contemporary design
C. Promote formulaic design solutions through the delivery of 'tickbox architecture' and 'standards-based urbanism'

Focussed more on process-related issues with an economic impact on the development process, a second set of critiques opined that design codes would:

D. Lead to excessively bureaucratic decision-making with less discretion and more paperwork and delay
E. Result in a cost-cutting culture through the exclusion of designers from the development process
F. Result in very restrictive and prescriptive planning through which the freedom of the market would be curtailed

Clearly based on the in-built presumptions and professional mind-sets (tyrannies) discussed above, positions were taken early, and certainly before any empirical evidence from the pilot process was forthcoming Over the course of the two years of research that followed, the same arguments continued to be made, including from the Urban Task Force of Richard Rogers. Repeating the assertion that a side-effect of coding would be a reduction in professional design input, it argued: "Design quality is threatened by an excessive reliance on design codes rather than design professionals." (Urban Task Force 2005: 7)

3. THE RESEARCH FINDINGS

The research delivered a substantial evidence on which to base judgements about the potential of design codes (see Carmona *et al* 2006c for detailed findings). It showed that as a particularly robust form of design guidance, design codes can play a major role in delivering better places, and this should be the major motivation for opting to use them. They do this by 'fixing' and delivering the 'must have' urban elements that form the common and unifying urban framework for schemes. They provide synergy and integration, by ensuring that the parts amount to a larger whole. This was a particularly strong finding among the 'advanced' case studies, where the built results on the ground provided tangible evidence of outcomes exceeding market norms.

They also have a significant role to play in delivering a more certain development process, and – when well managed – provide the focus around which teams of professional stakeholders can coordinate their activities in the process, delivering a more integrated and consensus driven development process. In one 'advanced' case study, for example, the line-up of key stakeholders included nineteen key groups including everything from the landowner to marketing and cost consultants. To achieve this, however, design codes require a significant up-front investment in time and resources from all parties, although the evidence suggested that for commercial interests this was compensated by the enhanced economic value that better design and a stronger sense of place could deliver (again, a finding common to all the 'advanced' case studies).

Interestingly the use of design codes made no discernable difference to the duration of the formal planning process (a key objective of Government was to streamline planning). However, as pay back for the up-front investment, a streamlined process of applying for and obtaining detailed 'reserved matters' consents for successive development phases was apparent, following the granting of an initial outline permission for the development as a whole.

The research concluded therefore that – in appropriate circumstances – design codes are valuable tools to deliver a range of more sustainable processes and built development outcomes. They are, however, just one possibility among a range of detailed design guidance options and it is important to understand where they should and should not be used. They are, for example, not normally of value for small sites, or where only one developer and design team is involved, and are of most valuable when sites possess one or more of the following characteristics:

– Large sites (or multiple smaller, related sites) that will be built out over a long period of time
– Sites in multiple ownership
– Sites likely to be developed by different developers and/or design teams

This reflects the key benefit of design codes (confirmed by the research) – namely their ability to coordinate the outputs of multiple teams and development phases across large sites to realise a coherent design vision.

Delivering new development entails a series of linked but often disparate processes. Design codes have a potential role to play in each, but more than that, they can provide an integrating focus through which to bring together the various processes and those involved in them. They do this because their preparation necessitates engaging all creative, market and regulatory parties early in these linked processes, with the resulting detailed discussions helping to resolve issues that otherwise typically cause tensions later in the development and undermine the quality of the built outcome:

– *Design processes* – design codes set the detailed urban design parameters of projects across the different scales of design intervention, from street and block sizes and layouts to landscape and architectural concerns, to help achieve a co-ordinated vision of place
– *Development processes* – design codes provide a means through which stakeholders can explore and negotiate detailed design options, and allow these concerns to feed into costing models and development options from an early stage
– *Planning processes* – design codes provide a ready means to consider, establish and adopt design parameters in a more objective manner, and then to regulate and monitor design solutions through the development control process
– *Adoption processes* – design codes allow adoption considerations (e.g. public sector adoption of highways, open space and drainage), to be coordinated at an early stage with design, development and planning matters, providing explicit standards for rigorous enforcement where necessary

The research, however, also showed design codes do not sit in isolation and are not a panacea for delivering better quality development – the need is also for good design codes and for rigorous coding processes in which the role of coding within the wider design, development and planning processes is fully considered (see DCLG 2006a for a detailed discussion). Moreover, if the commitment to their production and use is lacking amongst any key stakeholders, codes can become a divisive force and an expensive waste of resources. A number of pre-requisites are thus necessary for successful coding:

1. A coding team needs to be in place with the requisite design skills and leadership to drive the coding process forward
2. Stakeholders need to be prepared to make an up-front investment in time and resources
3. A commitment to design quality is needed both across the team and between public and private stakeholders
4. The code should deliver on the basis of a strong site-based vision (typically a master plan)

Rebutting the critiques

Returning to the critiques outlined above, the research demonstrated that design codes are not without problems – logistical, resource, skills and time-based. As with other forms of detailed design guidance, if design codes are themselves poorly designed, or inappropriately used, they will be as much part of the problem as the solution. Despite this, evidence from across the pilot programme, supported from a range of international experiences (Australia, Germany, Netherlands, USA – see Carmona & Dann 2007), suggested the arguments against codes are based on a range of common misconceptions.

Taking the group of critiques that broadly reflect a creative tyranny perspective (A to C above), far from stifling the creativity of designers, design codes were shown to have the potential to increase creative input into the development process. Whereas much volume house building in the UK has occurred without the input of architects and urban designers (Adam 1997), design codes (and the master plans to which they relate) cannot be prepared without these skills. Moreover, while some of the design codes examined strongly favoured traditional architectural design, others demonstrated that coding is equally suited to deliver innovative contemporary housing design.

The research revealed that design codes encourage delivery of a stronger and more unified sense of place, including architectural variety within a theme, and – critically – require that developers depart from standard house types, local municipalities and crude local development standards. They do this by encouraging stakeholders to think together about each development in its entirety as a specific place, then fixing this through the codes, rather than as a series of separate and discordant parts.

This integration of activity extends to the second set of critiques (D to F above), which broadly reflect a market tyranny perspective. The research revealed that rather than adding to and complicating the bureaucratic burden, when used correctly, codes can clarify regulatory processes and reduce the uncertainty faced by developers. In part this is because codes also reduce the discretion available to regulators by establishing and tying down the critical design components of schemes well in advance of detailed planning applications being received. In turn, this considerable investment up-front in the design process ensures that far from representing cost-cutting devices, design codes cannot be prepared without a significant injection of design time, skills and resources early in the process alongside the positive engagement of key stakeholders. As such they add to, rather than reduce, the overall design input into schemes,

	Spatial vision	Code design	Parcel design
Typical volume house building process			
Detailed masterplanning process			
Masterplan followed by design code process			

Note: Creative design input indicated by the size of circle

3 Design input and development processes compared

but also require additional resources to fund this (consultants fees ranged from £25K to £100K).

In fact design codes require the exercise of advanced design skills throughout the process of their preparation and use. Unlike other processes of development, coding distributes the creative input across three distinct phases of design – establishing the spatial design vision (typically a master plan), coding that vision, and designing each parcel as they come forward against the code. [3]

The quality of the final development is therefore dependent upon the quality of the site-based spatial vision (and the skills of the master planner), the quality of the code itself (and the skills of the code designer), and the quality of the parcel or scheme design (and the skills of the scheme designer). This compares favourably with other design intensive approaches such as development based solely on a detailed master plan where the design work is split between two phases of design (see CABE 2004b). It also marks a major advance on what has been the dominant model for large-scale residential development in the UK, where the basic design parameters are established to gain outline planning permission after which a specialist layout designer prepares detailed 'reserved matters' schemes based on standard units and technical development standards (POS *et al* 1998).

The codes were not uniformly prescriptive, restricting in the process the designer and/or developer's room for manoeuvre (a major concern of both creative and market critics). The case studies suggested local circumstances and the vision of those responsible for each code's design determines the precise characteristics of design codes. The case study code documents, for example, varied in length between 25 and 100 pages. While some aspects were highly prescriptive (e.g. building lines), others were dealt with much more flexibly (e.g. architectural treatments).

The extent to which codes are capable of modification during their life was also a matter for local decision, with formal processes of code review or the issuing of code supplements common in order to give greater flexibility between development phases and to enhance those parts of codes that proved less success-ful. Reflecting the balance that needs to be struck, Walters (2007: 94–5) warns: "The fear is always that codes will become overly prescriptive, but the experience shows that if codes back away from the levels of prescription necessary to achieve urban order and clarity in spatial layout, they run the real danger of becoming too flexible and allowing bad design to flourish alongside more creative interpretations."

Mediating the tyrannies

What is universal, however, is the potential for code production to act as a collaborative capacity building process and, in so doing, to challenge the types of praxis that underpin the three tyrannies. Thus, the research programme showed how coding brings together a wide range of individuals and organisations with a part to play in delivering development, and that these roughly divide into two groups: the 'coding team', which comprises the full range of technical stakeholders (professionals) involved in producing and using the code; and, 'wider interests', such as the local community. [4]

The coding team can be further divided into four sets of interests – land, design, development and public interests – while a critical role of successful coding processes is in providing the space for this range of stakeholders to understand and engage with the intersecting roles and prime motivations of all the others – in building trust and capacity within the team. These motivations varied across the case studies, but collectively included:

– The delivery of high quality design to support the creation of sustainable places – the primary objective

– Optimising investment returns – a necessary precondition

– Creating certain and efficient development process to facilitate the necessary investment

– Delivering planned development capacities (e.g. numbers of housing units and associated uses)

– Achieving key technical design parameters, whilst avoiding their over-dominance in design outcomes

– Establishing consensus over development, by delivering on all of the above

Groups	Interests	Stakeholders	Key stakeholder roles include
Coding Team	Land interests	Landowner	Establishing aspirations from the start for a high quality development, using freehold rights throughout to guarantee delivery against the design code
		Master-developer	Initiating the site-based vision and code design process through appointment of high quality designers, and subsequently assessing parcel development proposals against the code
		Funding agency	Using landownership and funding powers to deliver the requisite skills, resources and know-how for a high quality coding process, and effective assessment and enforcement
	Design interests	Masterplanner/ framework designer	Preparing the masterplan or development framework as a strong vision for the long-term development of a site(s), reflecting any existing policy and guidance, local consensus on the vision and the client's brief
		Code designer	Coordinating different interests as a basis to prepare the design code as a means to implement the essential principles contained in the masterplan / vision
	Development interests	Parcel developers	Developing proposals and achieve consents to deliver on site a development parcel within the masterplan / vision
		Social housing providers	If involved, developing proposals and achieve consents for the delivery on site of a development parcel – or part thereof – within the masterplan / vision
		Parcel designers	Creatively interpreting the code and masterplan to develop high quality designs for individual land parcels and their constituent buildings, spaces and areas
	Public interests	Planning authority	Establishing aspirations from the start for a high quality development, initiating or playing a role in initiating the masterplan / vision and design code, and administering the development control and any enforcement processes on the basis of the code
		Highways authority	Playing a role in design code production, revising and updating existing highways standards as necessary, and assessing and adopting the infrastructure that results
		Environment agency	Approving discharge from drainage facilities (i.e. sustainable urban drainage – SUDS), and advice on incorporation in the design code
		Building control	Approving parcel proposals against the national building regulations, and advice on incorporation and adaptation for the design code
Wider interests	Private interests	Utilities providers (including water)	Adopting service infrastructure, and advice on incorporation of requirements in the design code
	Community interests	Local politicians	Establishing design aspirations in advance of development interest, approving masterplan / vision and design code and delegating authority to officers to manage the delivery
		Existing community	Engaging in the masterplanning / vision making process through serious and significant involvement
		Future occupiers	Involvement through normal planning processes and engagement in long-term management and maintenance processes on the basis of the design code

4 Stakeholders roles within a typical coding process

To succeed, coding processes must address these collective aspirations. While key land and public interests, such as planning, are likely to be involved in one way or another from the start, others, such as parcel developers or highways authorities, will only be involved later on. It is thus imperative that those involved from the outset establish a firm basis upon which to work with other parties as they join the process further down the line. The pilot schemes suggested this can best be done when all parties collectively consider and address the full range of motivations from the start, and where this did not happen tensions arose.

Not every scheme subject to a design code follows the same process. Whether, for example, public or private sector stakeholders lead the process may determine who takes which role within the coding team. Certain roles can also be combined in single stakeholders, for instance: local authorities with appropriate skills in-house may take on the role of code designer;

landowners may act as the master-developer; and the master-developer may subsume the role of parcel developer. Design roles can also be combined. In some of the case studies the master plan (vision) designer was often the same person as the designer of the code.

An early and vital role of any coding process thus involves putting together the right team with the right skills and resources and commitment to the use of a coded approach. This process avoids selecting stakeholders stuck in the sorts of confrontational mindsets discussed above. Instead, stakeholders are selected who are willing and able to negotiate their role and contributions to the development process within the confines established by the code. Design codes thereby establish a zone within which productive negotiation (rather than compromise) occurs, internalising this within the development team rather than externalising it as open conflict. Tyranny is thereby replaced by understanding and a desire to address collective aspirations. [1]

Many minds remain set

Despite evidence from the research, many minds remained set, including some signature architects with their headline-generating potential. Will Alsop quickly proclaimed that: "Design codes will stifle our imagination." Similarly, Richard Rogers claimed: "Codes are for pen-pushers and penny-pinchers who have not a clue about design and want to find their way through the planning system." (quoted in Bennett 2005). On the market side, while recognising the potential of codes, too, for example, 'level-the-playing-field' between developers (Paul Newman of Paul Newman Homes quoted in English Partnerships 2007: 3), representatives of the real estate professions continued to express concern about the potential of such detailed guidance to reflect commercial considerations, to be flexible in the face of demand issues, and to speed up the development process (Barnes 2004).

A survey of architects attitudes to regulation generally confirmed these predominantly negative associations with design coding, with 39 per cent of architects recording hostility to their further use and 38 per cent being agnostic (Street 2007: 11). Clearly these historic confrontational mindsets are difficult to dislodge, the danger being that such architects will exclude themselves from the volume house building market for another generation.

Despite this, a minority of architects have been open to their use (22 per cent in the survey above), and despite an earlier Royal Institute of British Architects (RIBA) Practice Note that urged caution on the use of design codes and warned: "Design codes risk pattern-book housing" (RIBA 2005), following the launch of the research described in this chapter, the then RIBA President concluded that: "In the right circumstances and with the right expertise, they can speed up the planning process and deliver excellent results" (quoted in Bennett 2005). The architecture profession's division on this subject was, however, further illustrated when the RIBA changed their position yet again, and at the initiative of the subsequent president argued that codes would be a "dead hand to innovation." (Gates 2006)

4. CONCLUSION

No one sets out to create poorly laid out, characterless places, nor to exclude good designers from the residential development process, nor to prevent developers making a reasonable return on their investment. Despite this, too much of what has been built in the recent past displays the former characteristics, while the latter perceptions remain widespread among affected groups. As the research referred to in this lecture suggests, site-specific design codes have great potential to assist in overcoming these problems, with potential benefits including:

– Better designed development, with less opposition locally, and a level playing field for developers

- The enhanced economic value that a positive sense of place and better quality design can bring
- A more certain planning process and an associated more certain climate for investment
- A more coordinated development process built on consensus instead of conflict

Furthermore, in regulating future urban development, design coding does not stifle the potential for creativity and value generation, and may even enhance these critical contributions to place-making.

Multi-stakeholder site-based codes can thus help to bridge the gap between creative, market-driven, and regulatory modes of praxis – the three tyrannies. In doing so they are not simply regulatory tools for the control of private interests by public ones, or even of some private interests (developers) by others (land-owners), but are also tools for guidance and consensus building within a zone of productive negotiation rather than one of conflict and compromise. Design coding provides a medium through which to shake off narrow sectoral perspectives – the tyrannies – and in the process force the creators of the built environment to see the process as a collective and holistic endeavour.

Some stakeholders will never – for largely ideological reasons – accept any form of regulation as a positive contribution to the development process, but the empirical evidence shows that design codes have the potential to overcome the tyrannies by setting the development process within a far more positive context of productive negotiation. This is significant because it demonstrates how within a complex multi-stakeholder development process, it is still possible to deliver on creative and value agendas while successfully regulating the essentials of urban form and building understanding and capacity within the development team.

The reality of design codes thus differed from many assumptions, a reality seen in many of the most interesting English housing developments in recent years, including Hulme (Manchester), Greenwich Millennium Village (London), Newhall (Harlow), and Upton (Northampton). Although not universally praised, these developments (all case studies in the research reported here) represent major steps forward from the standard volume-built developments that would have been the alternative. A similar experience is evident in the US (see Parolek *et al* 2008: Section 4). It is thus possible to conclude that when used in the manner described above, design codes can be valuable tools to positively regulate the essentials of urbanism, while still leaving room for design creativity and enhanced market value.

For its part, the research demonstrated that eminent architects and developers (including national volume builders) have been willing to contribute to successive phases of projects within the schema laid down by design codes and despite initial reservations, have afterwards overwhelmingly given a strong endorsement to the process (Carmona et al 2006a: 15). As Elizabeth Plater-Zyberk (in Case Sheer & Preiser 1994: VII) has argued, "[…] control and freedom can co-exist most effectively when incorporated in regulations that precede the act of design, framing parameters of a given programme, rather than conflicting in judgement exerted on the completed design." As the experience of design coding suggests, whether in creative, market or regulatory roles, stakeholders benefit profoundly from positive engagement with each other. In the UK, recognition of the potential of design codes is now reflected in their adoption in government policy (DCLG 2006b: Annex B).

References

Adam R (1997) The Consumer, The Developer, The Architect and the Planner: Whose Design is Good?, paper given to the Good Design in Speculative Housing Seminar, London, Royal Fine Art Commission

Barnes Y (2004) Design Codes, The Implications for Landowners and Developers, paper given to the HBF Annual Design Conference, London

Bateman A (1995) Planning in the 1990s, A Developer's Perspective, Report, No. 1, February, pp. 26–9

Bennet E (2005) Prescott: What Urban Task Force? Building Design, No. 1702, 9 December, p. 2

Ben-Joseph E (2005) The Code of the City: Standards and the Hidden Language of Place Making, Cambridge Mass., MIT Press

Bentley I (1999) Urban Transformations: Power, People and Urban Design, London, Routledge

Burdette J (2004) Form-Based Codes: A Cure for the Cancer Called Euclidean Zoning?, unpublished Masters dissertation, Blacksburg VA, Virginia Polytechnic Institute

Carmona M (1998) "Design Control: Bridging the Professional Divide – Part 1: A New Framework" Journal of Urban Design, Vol. 3, No. 2, pp. 175–200

Carmona M (2001) Housing Design Quality: Through Policy, Guidance and Review, London, E & FN Spon

Carmona M (2006) "Practice Note: Designing Mega-projects in Hong Kong: Reflections from an Academic Accomplice", Journal of Urban Design, Vol. 11, No. 1, pp. 105–124

Carmona M, Carmona S & Gallent N (2003) Delivering New Homes: Processes, Planners and Providers, London, Routledge

Carmona M, de Magalhaes C & Edwards M (2001) The Value of Urban Design, London, Thomas Telford

Carmona M, de Magalhaes C & Hammond L (2008) Public Space, The Management Dimension, London, Routledge

Carmona M, Blum R, Hammond L, Stevens Q, Dann, J, Karski A, Pittock C, Rowlands S, Stille K (2006a) Design Coding in Practice, An Evaluation, London, Department for Communities and Local Government

Carmona M, Marshall S & Stevens Q (2006b) "Design Codes, Their Use and Potential", Progress in Planning, Vol. 65, No. 4

Carmona M & Dann J (2007) (Eds) "Design Codes" Urban Design Issue 101, Winter, pp. 16–35

Case Scheer B & Preiser W (1994) Design Review, Challenging Urban Aesthetic Control, New York Chapman & Hall

Colomb C (2007) Unpacking New Labour's 'Urban Renaissance' Agenda: Towards a Socially Sustainable Reurbanization of British Cities"? Planning Practice and Research, Vol. 22, No. 1, pp. 1–24

Commission for Architecture and the Built Environment (CABE) (2003) The Use of Urban Design Codes. Building Sustainable Communities, London, CABE

Commission for Architecture and the Built Environment (CABE) (2004a) Design Coding, Testing its Use in England, London, CABE

Commission for Architecture and the Built Environment (CABE) (2004b) Creating Successful Masterplans, A Guide for Clients, London, CABE

Commission for Architecture and the Built Environment (CABE) (2007a) Housing audit: assessing the design quality of new housing in the East Midlands, West Midlands and the South West, London, CABE

Commission for Architecture and the Built Environment (CABE) (2007b) A Sense of Place, What Residents Think of their New Homes, London, CABE

Cullen G (1961) Townscape, London, Architectural Press

Cullingworth B (1999) British Planning, 50 Years of Urban and Regional Policy, The Athlone Press, London

Department for Communities and Local Government (DCLG) (2006a) Preparing Design Codes, A Practice Manual, DCLG, London

Department for Communities and Local Government (DCLG) (2006b) Planning Policy Statement (PPS) 3: Housing, DCLG, London

Department for Communities and Local Government (DCLG) (2006c) Design Coding in Practice, An Evaluation, DCLG, London

Dittmar H (2005) Your Place or Mine? RIBA Journal, Vol. 113, No. 7, pp. 26–7

Duany A, Plater-Zyberk E & Speck J (2000) Suburban Nation, The Rise of Sprawl and the Decline of the American Dream, New York, North Point Press

Ellis C (200[The New Urbanism: Critiques and Rebuttals, Journal of urban Design, Vol. 7, No. 3, pp. 261–291

English Partnerships (2007) Design Codes, The English Partnerships Experience, London, English Partnerships

Fainstein S & Gladstone D (1997) 'Tourism and urban transformation: Interpretations of urban tourism', in O Källtorp, I Elander, O Ericsson and M Franzén (eds.),

Cities in Transformation – Transformation in Cities: Social and symbolic change of urban space, Aldershot: Ashgate, 119–135

Gardiner J (2004) The Codemaker, in Housing Today, 23 January 2004, pp. 26–28

Gates C (2006) RIBA Warns Over Design Codes, Building Design, No. 1712, 10 March, p. 6

Glancy J (2008) Architecture Deformed by Cash, Building Design, No. 1822, 6 June, p. 28

Hall P (2000) 'Creative cities and economic development', Urban Studies, Vol. 37 (4), pp. 639–649

Hebbert M (1998) London. More by Fortune than by Design. Chichester: John Wiley & Son

Heriot-Watt University, School of the Built Environment (2007) Design at the Heart of House-Building, Edinburgh, The Scottish Government

Housebuilders' Federation (HBF) & Royal Institute of British Architects (RIBA) Good Design in Housing, London HBF

Imrie R & Street E (2006) Papers in 'The Codification and Regulation of Architects' Practices', Project Paper 3, The Attitudes of Architects Towards Planning Regulation and Control, London, Kings College London

Lang J (2005) Urban Design, A Typology of Procedures and Products, Oxford, Architectural Press

Mantownhuman (2008) Manifesto: Towards a New Humanism in Architecture, www.mantownhuman.org

McGlynn S (1993) 'Reviewing the Rhetoric' in Making Better Places, Urban Design Now, Hayward R & McGlynn S (eds), Oxford, Architectural Press

Ministry for the Environment (2005) New Zealand Urban Design Protocol, http://www.mfe.govt.nz/issues/urban/design-protocol/index.html

Office for the Deputy Prime Minister (ODPM) (2003) Sustainable Communities, Building for the Future, http://www.communities.gov.uk/communities/sustainablecommunities/sustainablecommunities/

Office for the Deputy Prime Minister (ODPM) (2005) The Future for Design Codes, Further Information to Support Stakeholders Reading Draft PPS3, London, ODPM

Planning Officers' Society (POS), House Builders' Federation (HBF & the Department for Environment, Transport and the Regions (1998) Housing Layouts – Lifting the Quality, London, HBF

Parolek D, Parolek K & Crawford P (2008) Form-Based Codes, A Guide for Planners, urban Designers, Municiplities, and Developers, Hoboken New Jersey, John Wiley & Sons

Rand A (1993) The Fountainhead, New York, Signet

Reade E (1987) British Town and Country Planning, Open University Press, Milton Keynes

Royal Institute of British Architects (RIBA) (2005) RIBA Practice Bulletin: Design Codes Risk Pattern Book Housing, 2nd March, London, RIBA

Rowland I D & Howe T N (eds) (1999) Vitruvius. Ten Books on Architecture. Cambridge: Cambridge University Press

Rowley A (1998), 'Private-property decision makers and the quality of urban design', Journal of Urban Design, Vol. 3, No. 2, pp. 151–173

Savage R (2001) Planning for Acceptable Housing Development, unpublished MPhil Thesis, London, University College London

Southworth M & Ben Joseph E (1997) Streets and the Shaping of Towns and Cities. New York: McGraw-Hill

Smyth H (1994) Marketing the City: The role of flagship developments in urban regeneration, London, E & FN Spon

Street E (2007) Papers in 'The Codification and Regulation of Architects' Practices', Project Paper 5, The Use of Design Coding in England, London, Kings College London

Tiesdell S & Adams D (2004) Design Matters: Major House Builders and the Design Challenge of Brownfield Development Contexts

Urban Task Force (2005) Towards a Strong Urban Renaissance, http://www.urbantaskforce.org

Van Doren P (2005) The Political Economy of Urban Design Standards, in Ben-Joseph E & Szold T (Eds) Regulating Place, Standards and the Shaping of Urban America, London, Routledge, pp. 45–66

Walters D (2007) Designing Community, Charrettes, Masterplans and Form-based Codes, Oxford, Architectural Press

Wellings F (2006) British Housebuilders, History and Analysis, Oxford, Blackwell Publishing

Worpole K & Knox K (2007) The Social Value of Public Spaces, York, Joseph Rowntree Foundation

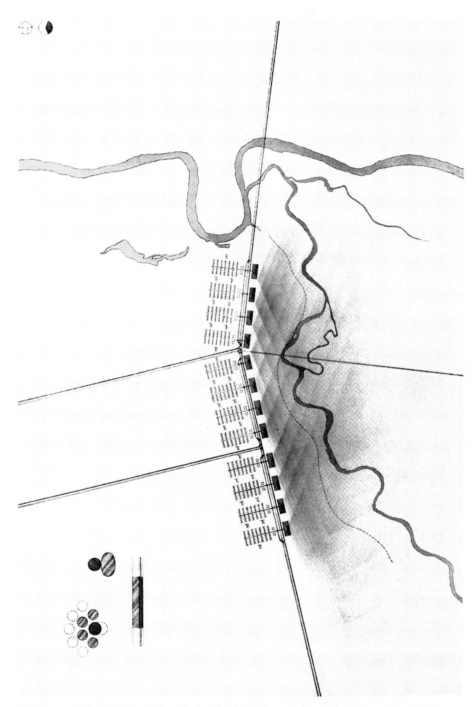

2 *"European industrial City" replanned with all industry downwind by Ludwig Hilberseimer, 1944 (Hilberseimer 1944).*

MICHAEL HEBBERT *Street Atmosphere*

The topic of street atmosphere seems especially topical in the season of Advent. As I headed for Manchester Airport en route to the Dortmunder Vorträge, crowds of people were streaming down the ramp from Piccadilly Railway Station towards the brightly lit shops and street markets of the city centre. Next day, catching the train out to the TU Dortmund campus, I met a similar throng crossing the Königswall and climbing the steps towards the Kampstraße. The pulling power of Christmas markets can't be measured by the usual criteria of retail attraction – it's the sensory atmosphere of lights, sights, smells, sounds and human warmth that draws the crowds to the streets of a city centre in the middle of winter.

Stadtbaukunst is, among other things, an atmospheric art. The urban designer manipulates many factors that contribute to the ambience of streets. They include the physical morphology through which buildings enclose and define urban space: the aesthetics of style, materials and colours; the scenography of building plans in perspective, offering sightlines to distant landmarks, and of interior spaces glimpsed through windows and openings; the furnishing of the public realm, its pavings, trees, kiosks, and lamp standards; sounds and smells; the movement patterns of everyday life. All these elements and more combine to make or erode the atmosphere of the street.

That's atmosphere in a metaphorical sense – but the street also has a literal atmosphere. It is comprised of invisible gas and can be measured by the meteorological parameters of radiation, temperature, humidity, wind, precipitation, and air quality. [1] The pattern of weather observations as they oscillate through the cycles of day and night, fronts and depressions, seasons and years, can be said to constitute a 'climate'. The microclimate of the street forms part of the mesoclimate of the town, which is quite distinct from that of the country landscape in which it is situated. The geometry of urban buildings redistributes solar radiance and disturbs the airflow of the winds, its impermeable surfaces repel moisture, its dense construction materials store heat, its dust and pollution intercept sunlight. From the perspective of climatology the streets and buildings of a town appear as an anomalous layer within the multi-level circulation system of the global atmosphere, a layer significantly affected by human emissions of warmth and pollutants, with a three-dimensional environment that traps radiation and transforms wind flow into complex turbulent patterns. The thermal experience of a town's human occupants is determined by its anthropogenically modified temperature, humidity and airflow. Since humans will generally take steps to avoid discomfort, street microclimate conditions behaviour. Amid all the warmth and light of a *Weihnachtsmarkt*, a stallholder would choose not to be selling *Glühwein* from a draughty pitch on the shady side of the square.

From 2010 to 2011 I undertook a research project entitled "Climate Science and Urban Design. A Historical and Comparative Perspective", with funding from the UK Economic and Social Research Council. My co-investigator was Vladimir Jankovic, a science historian who specializes in meteorology within CHSTM, the Centre for the History of Science, Technology and Medicine. Our collaboration was triggered by a conversation about two incidental discoveries. I had discovered from the voluminous footnotes of George and Christiane Collins's *Camillo Sitte: The Birth of Modern City Planning* (Collins 1988) that Sitte was as interested in the microclimate of streets as in the more metaphorical aspects of street atmosphere. His writings make several references to Vitruvius, whose theory of street alignment in *De Architectura libri decem* is based on wind direction, and he castigates "the sophisticated builders of modern cities" who have forgotten the ancient principles of design for sun and wind. Recalling that Le Corbusier was equally sure of his meteorological credentials from an antithetical design stance, it seemed to me that Vitruvianism might be an interesting and under-researched aspect of design history.

Meanwhile my colleague Vladimir Jankovic had discovered a similarly under-researched episode in the history of science, the attempt of post-war climatologists to apply their knowledge through urban design, using the architecture of the city to achieve desired climatic outcomes for thermal comfort and air quality. A seminal statement of this ambition was *Urban Climatology and its Relevance to Urban Design* published in 1976 as Technical Note 149 by the World Meteorological Organization – a document all the more interesting because its author Tony Chandler was Professor of Geography at our own University of Manchester.

We set out to research both sides of the equation – the science and the design – looking particularly at experiences since 1950, and at links to the topical concern with design for carbon mitigation and adaptation to the weather patterns of global climate change. The project involved extensive interviews and engagement with practitioners. The papers and proceedings can be viewed online at www.sed.manchester.ac.uk/architecture/research/csud/

Climatically-aware design is often called 'Vitruvian' because that's how Marcus Vitruvius Pollio approaches the topic of urban design in his classic treatise *De Architectura*, Chapter 1.6, "The Directions of the Streets: with remarks on the winds", calls for a Tower of the Winds – a marble *amussium* – to be set at the centre of a town-site and streets to be aligned exactly along the lines of division between the quarters of the various winds, so they strike against the angles of the blocks and their risk to health is broken and dispersed. Vitruvius was drawing upon long traditions of classical thinking about the microclimates of towns. The ancient treatise on "Airs, Waters, and Places" attributed to Hippocrates argues that healthy residents with good skin colour and clear voices live in cities exposed to the winds originating in the East, between the summer and winter risings of the sun; healthy positioning in relation to wind and sun comes before military security as the first principle of town layout in Aristotle's *Politics* IV.11; and the treatise on winds by Aristotle's favourite pupil Theophrastus of Eresus includes an appreciation of the effect of buildings and passages on airflow (Theophrastus of Eresus 1894: 36). Classical thinking echoes the sensibility of other ancient civilisations, such as the close appreciation of wind, water and physical setting in Chinese town plans, still echoed in feng shui design method.

De Architectura was rediscovered in the library of the Convent of St Gall around 1413. The manuscript contained one of the oldest surviving illustrations of a Roman treatise, a diagram of the winds drawn about 700 A.D. Besides its well-known influence on the classical revival in architecture, Vitruvian theory contributed significantly to the experimental geometries of Renaissance town planning. Wind roses became a habitual accompaniment of town maps, beginning (as Spiro Kostof notes) with Leonardo da Vinci's remarkable survey of the city of Imola in 1503. King Philip II of Spain showed a Vitruvian concern in the ordinances concerning the laying out of towns in the New World which he issued from the Escorial in 1573: town sites were to allow entrance and departure open to the north wind, and building lots and edifices to be arranged in such a manner that rooms might enjoy the best airs; in the middle of every town should be an oblong plaza aligned to break the force of the winds. Vitruvian theory of town layout reappeared as a significant consideration in response to the hyper-density and filth of the early industrial city. Fighting against the tide of *laissez-faire*, advocates of regulatory control over street layout appealed to the authority of *De Architectura* to justify measures that would ensure ventilation and free passage of "clean-sweeping breezes" (Hebbert 1999). So did all the parties in the late nineteenth century reform controversies between proponents of straight and curved streets.

In the interwar years the Modern Movement claimed the Vitruvian mantle in its polemic against the corridor street. Le Corbusier referenced the science of climatology in his drawings of wind eddies trapping the pollution within canyon streets, and medical science in his theory of "exact respiration" whereby the architect optimises insolation and abolishes stale air (Le Corbusier 1967: 40–50). The central claim of the *Charter of Athens* was that the "three imperious necessities" of space, sun and ventilation could best be guaranteed within an radically simplified environment based on the functional components of housing, work, recreation and traffic. Within the Bauhaus Ludwig Hilberseimer was commissioned by Mies van der Rohe to perfect the orientation of dwellings in relation to through-ventilation and penetration of a minimum of four hours of direct sunlight at the winter solstice as part of the larger formulation of an *Existenzminimum*. From this single parameter and a prevailing wind direction Hilbersheimer arrived at the concept of the city as an indefinite multiplication of L-shaped dwellings on diagonal access roads in herring-bone patterns, spaced to ensure natural dispersion of air pollution from the adjacent industrial units (Hilberseimer 1944). [2]

Like many urbanists of the mid-twentieth century, Hilberseimer claimed to derive his hyper-rationalist theory of the Modern City from examination of historical urban forms (Hilberseimer 1955, Pommer 1988: 93– 113). Wolfgang Sonne and I have commented elsewhere (Hebbert and Sonne 2006) on this paradoxical cult of modernist historicism, which finds its

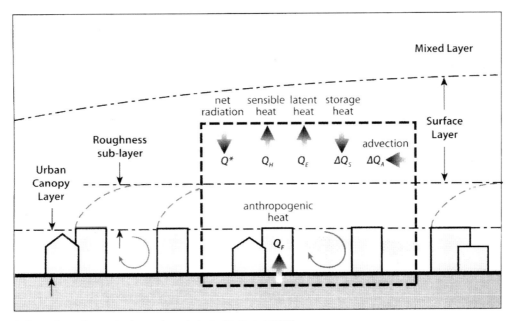

1 Street Atmosphere – the thermo-dynamic basis (Erell et al 2011).

climax in Ernst Egli's *Die Neue Stadt in Landschaft und Klima* (Egli 1951). Half of that book is about the New City, designed from first principles as a combination of functional zones linked by a modern traffic circulation, with buildings raised on pilotis "[…] while the whole surface of our dear earth, passing uninterrupted beneath the buildings, is given back to the pedestrian" (Egli 1951: 21). But the other half, beautifully illustrated with aerial photography from the Swissair survey collection, shows the subtle variety with which traditional settlements of Europe and Asia have responded to diverse geographical contexts, schematized as six climatic zones and seven basic types of topographical setting. In a ludicrous conclusion, Egli attempts to reconcile the universal formula of Die Neue Stadt with the demands of context in almost indistinguishable versions of a kilometre-square neighbourhood of 11-storey blocks (each of 330 apartments), one for a hot dry climate, and the other for a subarctic setting.

Unfortunately, the attempt to formulate a climatic *Existenzminimum* was based on erroneous science. Designers were looking for universal formulae that could be coded and reproduced for mass production, but the trend of scientific discovery was towards recognition of spatial specificity and fine-grained variation in urban microclimates. Albert Kratzer's *Stadtklima* was the seminal text, synthesizing a mass of previously disconnected monographs. It showed how the climatic structure of towns has to be studied at three distinct scales: the urban heat island as a whole, with its pollution plume, characteristic wind system, precipitation pattern, and downwind shadow effect; the distinct mesoclimates of urban functional areas and neighbourhoods; and thirdly the mosaic of individual streets, each having its own climatic profile, depending upon alignment with respect to sun and wind, height, width, vegetation, building materials and the multitude of factors that constitute urban design. Published in 1937, *Stadtklima* stimulated worldwide interest in the phenomenon of street atmospheres. By

the time of Kratzer's second edition in 1956 a wave of scientific publication had boosted his reference list from 225 papers to 533. A WMO bibliography of urban climatology published by Tony Chandler in 1970 contained 1,800 references. American interest developed strongly, with funding from the US military and remarkably effective academic leadership in the person of Helmut Landsberg, a German-trained meteorologist who had emigrated from Frankfurt am Main in 1931. Landsberg had a key role as Director of Climatology with the US Weather Bureau from 1954, and was influential in promoting urban climatology at a global level through the World Meteorological Organisation from its foundation in 1950 right up to his death (in Geneva) in 1985. One of his most famous experiments was the observation campaign that accompanied the construction of the new town of Columbia in the state of Maryland (Landsberg 1979). Before the start of building works in 1968 he installed meteorological instruments across the farmland site, and monitored them over seven years as the town was constructed and the population grew from 200 to 20,000. The anthropogenic effect of urbanisation upon climate was vividly demonstrated in rising run-off, falling humidity and wind speed, and the appearance of a heat island with a nocturnal differential of 8°C.

Landsberg was vividly aware of the relevance of this field of scientific enquiry to the practice of urban design. He coupled the evidence of urbanisation's adverse climatic effects with the growing urbanisation trend worldwide. In a prophetic contribution to a Renner-Glenn symposium on climate change published in 1970, he noted the evidence that the planet's energy balances had already been inadvertently tipped by the greenhouse effect of CO_2 emissions: but whereas the global CO_2 balance was still at an early stage of scientific investigation, scientists already had a good quantitative understanding of the anthropogenic effects of man's activities on the urban microclimate — they were pronounced, far-reaching and increasingly alarming (Landsberg 1970: 1270). He said of the standard US model of low-density suburbanisation, with its buildings dependent on energy-intensive heating in winter and air conditioning in summer, and its heat-absorbent public realm of impervious paving and asphalt: "[…] consciously or otherwise such developments violate every climatic principle, producing a microclimate much like that of a desert" (Landsberg 1947: 117).

As prolific communicator, Landsberg challenged both his scientific colleagues to see urban climatology as an applied science, and planners and architects to apply it: good examples are the paper "Microclimatology" in the *Architectural Record* of July 1947, and *Weather, Climate and Human Settlements* (Landsberg 1976) written as a Special Environmental Report for WMO, and his book *The Urban Climate* (Landsberg 1981) written explicitly as a successor to Kratzer's seminal *Stadtklima*. Much of his international activity focussed on bridge-building between climate scientists and the design professions. As chair of the Commission for Applied Climatology he stimulated a series of cross-discipline collaborations between WMO, the World Health Organisation, the International Federation for Housing and Town Planning, the International Society for Biometeorology and the Confédération Internationale du Bâtiment which continued after his death, culminating in the International Association for Urban Climate (Hebbert and MacKillop 2013). By contrast with the Vitruvianism of Camillo Sitte and the bold, if erroneous, promises of the *Ville Radieuse*, the late twentieth century history encounter between climatology and urbanism was a dialogue of the deaf, remarkable in its failure, with some honourable exceptions in the German-speaking countries, where *Stadtklima* did keep a place in town-planning education and practice. The topic of climate continued to be largely ignored until the turn of the 21st century, when incontrovertible evidence of global climate change on the global scale prompted a revival of interest in the atmospheric environment at the urban scale (Hebbert and Jankovic 2013).

This lacuna can be explained in various ways. The introduction of air pollution regulation and smoke controls removed much of the visual evidence of contamination from street atmospheres. Increasing reliance on motor vehicles and air conditioning diminished awareness of the open-air environment. In the context of the post-war welfare state, planning's concern with social relations had eclipsed its earlier interest in the physical environment. Urban design drew upon the visual cultures of architecture and heritage conservation and was almost entirely silent on environmental matters. For its part, the environmental management movement was anti-urban in spirit, and had little interest in the microclimates of those mineral canyons, city streets.

There was also a more fundamental epistemological problem. The emerging science of urban climatology was difficult to translate into rules of action. Certain though it is that design affects climate, the causality is not straightforward. In texts written by climate specialists for design practitioners – for example Baruch Givoni's *Climate Considerations in Building and Urban Design* (Givoni 1998) or *Urban Climate, Designing Spaces between Buildings* by Evyatar Erell and colleagues (Erell 2011) – almost every statement has to be qualified by a 'however' or an 'on the other hand'. Helmut Landsberg illustrated the difficulty with the apparently obvious rule of arranging a settlement so that its pollution is dispersed on the prevailing wind. Ludwig Hilberseimer, as we have seen, assumed this to be the fundamental axiom of all urban spatial organisation. But as Landsberg pointed out, "using the so-called prevailing wind direction […] is a poor use of meteorological information indeed. Planning should proceed with the wind directions that are associated with a meteorological stagnation condition. The light winds that permit accumulations of pollutants rarely coincide with the 'prevailing' wind directions." (Landsberg 1976, 20)

For example in Sydney, New South Wales, the industrial pollution carried out to sea on the prevailing winds is carried back into the city each morning on the light sea breeze (Douglas 1983); in Munich the critical winds for atmospheric pollution are not the common westerlies but the slow-moving airflow from the east which affords ventilation during climatic inversions in summer months (Matzarakis and Mayer 1992). The message of the wind rose is one of diurnal and seasonal variation in wind directions, velocities and temperatures, and its pattern varies from site to site according to topography and built form. Most towns have an internal wind system in which air from the cooler surrounding landscape is drawn inwards towards the centre of the urban heat island from all points of the compass. Hills and valleys can block or divert winds, and high ground often forms a reservoir of denser cool air that pours down through the streets and open spaces by gravity. Sea, lakes, rivers and parks all affect the street atmosphere and every cluster of buildings – in aerodynamic terms, the 'roughness layer' – has a unique three-dimensional configuration and associated turbulence pattern.

Now, the language of urbanism tends to be based on codes or pattern languages. Cities are built by a repetitive process of multiplication and the most effective planning principles are those that can be codified. The movement for passive and low energy architecture (PLEA) progressed because many of the factors in building performance – sunlight angles, direction of water flow, thermal performance of standard building materials – are straightforwardly predictable. By contrast, the outdoor atmosphere of the street is a complex *Gestalt*, unique to its location, and requiring site-*specific* diagnosis.

Landsberg recognised these contradictions when he tried in 1972 to formulate a blueprint for "Metutopia", a meteorologically optimised town design. He laid out basic ground rules for town planners: for example, not to build on floodplains, maximise green cover and tree planting to mitigate the urban heat island, minimise surface parking lots, design compactly, capture waste heat through district heating schemes and use it to melt snows in northern climates, develop non-polluting alternatives to the private automobile and ban toxic fuel additives, and so forth. But his final ground

rule marks the limits of generalisation about street atmosphere. What the designers of Metutopia need above all is local knowledge of their site: topographic and synoptic conditions vary widely, so do low-level temperature lapse rates, wind speeds, ventilation rates, and inversion effects – the well-designed city, in other words, is one whose planners have specific climatic information on the air resource for which they are planning (Landsberg 1973: 89).

Yet such information has not been easy to procure. Mainstream meteorological services are oriented towards weather forecasting and the requirements of the aviation and agricultural industries, and the military. The synoptic weather models – on which all forecasting is based – are based on grids too large-scale to resolve the particularities of urban climate. Most weather stations are intentionally situated in open spaces such as parks or airports so as to avoid data-contamination from the 'urban anomaly'. Even where historic town centre observatories exist and have sufficient long-term data series for analysis of climate trends, they need to be supplemented by a network of other stations, closely-spaced enough to explore the internal dynamics of the urban heat island. In-depth investigations of urban climate such as the *Stadtluft München* project (Matzarakis and Mayer 1992) or Stanley Changnon's METROMEX (Metropolitan Meteorological Experiment) in St Louis required special instrumentation and extended observation campaigns. Being expensive to mount, they rarely occurred. Consequently it is fair to say that even if twentieth century urbanists had been more inquisitive about the physical atmosphere of their streets, they would have found the information precious hard to obtain.

Since the millennium the picture has begun to change in three ways. First and most obviously, global climate change sets a different policy context for cities. Mayors have found themselves on the front line of storm surges, river flooding, heatwaves and blizzards. While international agreement on carbon mitigation has stalled, city decision-makers have woken up to the anthropogenic climate processes within their own boundaries, and their potential to mitigate global warming risk through adaptive strategies based on tree planting, albedo, permeable paving, water spaces and environmentally-informed design. Vitruvianism is on the agenda again.

Secondly, meteorological technology has been miniaturised by digital sensors that are cheaper, lighter and more flexible to install than the old thermometers, barometers and anemometers: weather stations streaming radio data from lamp posts or mounted on bicycles – as here in Rotterdam [3] – have cut the cost of observation. At the same, the numerical models used by urban climatologists have become at once more powerful and yet more accessible. They can accurately simulate weather outcomes with less requirement for verification. Using open-source software such as the ENVI-met programme developed by Michael Bruse of the University of Mainz, it is increasingly easy for researchers to simulate and explore the four-way interactions between buildings, vegetation, topography and atmosphere.

The third significant innovation comes from the coupling of urban climate models with three-dimensional digital models of urban areas, and with demographic and socio-economic data on a Geographical Information System (GIS) base. A good example is the *Digitale Umweltatlas Berlin*, which includes localised bioclimatic profiles of residents in their ambient environments, mapped at high-resolution and publicly available online. Berlin also provides *Bewertungskarten* (evaluation maps) identifying the climatic functions of urban spaces as generators of cold air, ventilation corridors, zones of air exchange and "bioclimatically stressed built-up areas". The accompanying text draws the corollary for planners and designers in terms of the siting, height and alignment of buildings. This Vitruvian combination of climate analysis with design guidelines has become known as the *Klimaatlas* approach. It was pioneered by the city of Stuttgart (Webb and Hebbert 2012), promulgated by the Verein Deutscher Ingenieure under National Guideline VDI-3787 *Environmental Meteorology Climate and Air Pollution Maps for Cities and Regions*, and is now being imitated by cities around the world,

3 Bicycle-mounted weather observatory of Prof. Bert Van Hove, Wageningen University.

4 Prof. Dr. Toshaki Ichinose with the Klimaatlas for Osaka.

especially in South East Asia (Ren at al 2011). One of the most interesting discoveries of our research project "Climate Science and Urban Design" was the extent to which Japanese cities have adopted the *Klimaatlas* technique, including its German name. In figure 4, for example, the leading climate modeller Toshiaki Ichinose of the National Institute for Environmental Studies in Tsukuba Science City displays the *Klimaatlas* for Osaka. Here we have exactly what Helmut Landsberg called for in 1972, a sophisticated, high-resolution analysis of the urban climate that shows architects and planners what they need to know in order to enhance street atmospheres, and what to avoid. The information cannot guarantee Metutopia but it is a vital step along the way.

To conclude: in their inspirational prologue – "to our readers" – of the first issue of the monthly magazine *Der Städtebau* in 1904, Camillo Sitte and Theodor Goecke celebrated the birth of modern urbanism as a multidimensional enterprise – artistic, cultural, hygienic, technical, social, and politico-economic. They explicitly included the need for urban space designers to understand the importance of humidity, temperature, air quality and ventilation. But climate awareness would prove the most elusive of all the many facets of *Städtebau* over the course of the twentieth century. It took a further hundred years for the science of anthropogenic weather effects at the urban scale to develop usable measurement and modelling tools, and find a spatially precise medium for presenting climatic information. At the same time, catastrophic anthropogenic alteration to global climate balances have created a fresh political context for planning. Previously indifferent decision-makers now want to know how the built environment aggravates or mitigates heat, cold, humidity and air movement. So we end with a paradox: shaping street atmosphere through design – Vitruvianism – is both the oldest idea in planning history and its newest challenge.

Acknowledgement

Research for the paper was funded exclusively by the Economic and Social Research Council under award ESRC RES 062-23-2134, „Climate Science and Urban Design, a Historical and Comparative Study".

References

Berlin Senatsverwaltung für Stadtentwicklung und Umwelt, *Karten zum Stadtklima* www.stadtentwicklung.berlin.de/umwelt/umweltatlas/dinh_04.htm (online resource, various dates).

T. Chandler, *Urban Climatology and its Relevance to Urban Design*, Geneva: World Meteorological Organisation, Geneva 1976.

G. R. Collins & C. C. Collins, *Camillo Sitte: the Birth of Modern City Planning*, New York 1986.

Le Corbusier, *La Ville Radieuse* [first published 1933], London 1967.

I. Douglas, *The Urban Environment*, London 1983.

E. Egli, *Die Neue Stadt in Landschaft und Klima*, Erlenbach, Zürich 1951.

E. Erell, D. Pearlmutter and T. Williamson, *Urban Microclimate: Designing the Spaces Between Buildings*, London 2011.

B. Givoni, *Man Climate and Architecture*, Amsterdam 1998.

M. Hebbert, "A City in Good Shape: Town Planning and Public Health" In: *Town Planning Review* 70, no. 4, pp. 433–454, 1999.

M. Hebbert & W. Sonne, "History Builds the Town: The Uses of History in Twentieth Century City Planning" pp. 3–20 in: F. Javier Monclús and Manuel Guàrdia (eds.), *Culture Urbanism and Planning*, Aldershot 2006.

M. Hebbert & F. Mackillop, "Urban Climatology Applied to Urban Planning: A Postwar Knowledge Circulation Failure" In: *International Journal of Urban and Regional Research*. DOI: 10.1111/1468-2427.12046, 2013.

M. Hebbert, V. Jankovic & B. Webb, *City Weathers: Meteorology and Urban Design 1950–2010*, University of Manchester, Manchester Architecture Research Centre, 2011. [ebook downloadable at: www.sed.manchester.ac.uk/architecture/research/csud/workshop/2011CityWeathers.pdf]

M. Hebbert & B. Webb, "Towards a Liveable Urban Climate – Lessons from Stuttgart" ch. 7 in C. Gossop & S. Nan (eds.), *Liveable Cities: Urbanising World* [ISOCARP 07] London & New York 2012.

L. Hilberseimer, *The New City: Principles of Planning*, Chicago 1944.

S. Kostof, *The City Assembled – The Elements of Urban Form Through History*, Boston, Massachusetts, 1992.

A. Kratzer, *Das Stadtklima*, Braunschweig 1937.

H. E. Landsberg, „Microclimatology" in: *Architectural Forum* 86.3, pp. 114–9, 1947.

H. E. Landsberg, "The Climate of Towns" in: W. L. Thomas (ed.), *Man's Role in Changing the Face of the Earth*, pp. 584–603, Chicago 1956.

H. E. Landsberg, "The Meteorologically Utopian City" In: *Bulletin of the American Meteorological Society*, 51, 2, pp. 86–9, 1973.

H. E. Landsberg, *Weather, Climate and Human Settlements*, Geneva 1976.

H. E. Landsberg, "Atmospheric Changes in a Growing Community (the Columbia Maryland Experience)" in *Urban Ecology* 4,1, pp. 53–81, 1979.

H. E. Landsberg, *The Urban Climate*, London 1981.

A. Matzarakis & H. Mayer, "Mapping Urban Air-paths for Planning in Munich" pp. 13–18 in: K. Höschele (ed.), *Planning Applications in Urban and Building Climatology*, Karlsruhe, Institut für Meteorologie ind Klimaforschung der Universität Karlsruhe, 1992.

R. Pommer, D. Spaeth & K. Harrington, *In The Shadow of Mies: Ludwig Hilberseimer, Architect Educator & Urban Planner*, New York 1988.

C. Ren, E. Y. Ng, L. Katzschner, "Urban climatic map studies, a review", in: *International Journal of Climatology* 31, 15, pp. 2213–2233, 2011.

Theophrastus of Eresus, *On Winds and on Weather Signs* [trans. J. G. Wood], London 1894.

Verband Region Stuttgart, *Klimaatlas Region Stuttgart*, Stuttgart 2008. [downloadable from www.stadtklima-stuttgart.de]

Plot-based urbanism: Murano.

SERGIO PORTA, OMBRETTA ROMICE *Plot-Based Urbanism*

Towards Time Consciousness in Place Making

"This quality in buildings and in towns cannot be made, but only generated, indirectly, by the ordinary actions of the people, just as a flower cannot be made, but only generated from the seed."

Christopher Alexander, 1980

1. INTRODUCTION: ON GIANTS' SHOULDERS

For those interested in urban design and planning these are exciting days. A whole new story is beginning in Scotland where at many levels the promise of a better world is raising from new forms of synergy between the agenda of sustainability for policy makers and that of place making for architects and urban scholars in general.

It took a while to reach this point. More than ten years ago, influential documents like *Towards an Urban Renaissance* (The Urban Task Force 1999) and *The Urban Design Compendium* (English Partnership and Housing Corporation 2000) inaugurated this new page by summarizing in form of guidelines a wealth of literature from the late 1980s which included works by Peter Newman and Jeff Kenworthy In Australia (Newman & Kenworthy 1999), Peter Calthorpe (Calthorpe & Fulton 2001) and Andres Duany (Krieger & Lennerz 1991) in the USA, Ian Bentley (McGlynn, Smith, Alcock, Murrain & Bentley 1985), Mike Jenks (Jenks & Burgess 2000) and Hildebrand Frey (Frey 1999) in the UK, and many others.

To be true, this new wave of urbanism, which took the names of New Urbanism in the USA and place making in the UK, proceeded on the shoulders of giants like Jane Jacobs (Jacobs 1961), Christopher Alexander (Alexander 1965), Gordon Cullen (Cullen 1965), Kevin Lynch (Lynch 1960), Oscar Newman (O. Newman 1973), Donald Appleyard and Allan Jacobs (Appleyard 1982; Jacobs & Appleyard 1987). These were protagonists of the first sharp criticism to the many facets of conventional urbanism in the early 1960s, still shrunk between endless sprawl and senseless 'towers-in-the-park'. Such two models of conventional urbanism stemmed directly from the theories of those masters of thought, like Ebenezer Howard (Howard 1902) and Le Corbusier (Corbusier 1923), who shaped the new discipline of urban planning and design at the very dawn of the 20th century.

However, contemporary challenges are such — in terms of scale, type and urgency — that a much deeper shift is needed in urban disciplines just to start dealing with them. [1] Some of us have recently argued that what we still miss is the serious consideration of the factor of time in urbanism, or, in other words, a deeper "time-conscious" approach (Thwaites, Porta, Romice & Greaves 2008). Inevitably, that means focusing on change as the essential dynamic of evolution in the built environment, which in turn leads to re-addressing concepts like control, self-organization and community participation. After time and change

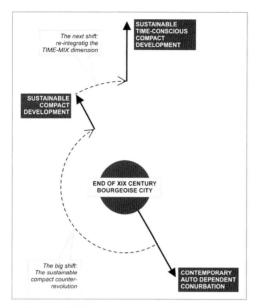

1 The big shift from conventional urbanism to the current place making or New Urbanism approach (the sustainable compact counter-revolution) and the need for a deeper shift towards a more time-conscious approach (Thwaites, Porta, Romice & Greaves 2008, p. 24).

have been finally firmly placed at the centre stage, the whole discipline of urban planning and design, its conceptual equipment as well as its operational toolbox, reveals its weaknesses under a new light and calls for the construction of a different scenario.

This paper poses the problem of this scenario in disciplinary terms; it argues about its premises and outlines its essential features. The scope of this paper is not to deliver a comprehensive model for a new approach to urban planning and design, but to set the right framework and rise the right questions so that we can start thinking of issues such as urban regeneration, informal settlements and massive urbanization, community participation and representation, beauty and humanity in space, in a different way.

This doesn't necessarily means starting from scratch. We should not be obsessed by the quest for a new approach – like too often happened in the past; we should, instead, restlessly search for a right approach. Our reflection leads to concepts like 'urban seeding' and 'plot-based urbanism' that are inherently based

on evidence coming from what we see on the ground as a manifestation of evolution through time: change embeds levels of permanency as well as of innovation, universality as well as specificity. Distinguishing between these levels is all-important if change has to be finally understood and inform our action on the ground.[1]

2. URBAN SEEDING: THE CASE FOR A DIFFERENT DISCIPLINE

2.1. Sprawl and Towers-in-the-Park: Overcoming the Cultural Problem

It is a long story indeed. A story dense of intellectual challenges and adventurous human trajectories that sometimes resulted in sharp conflicts with each other. It was also a story of major failures. The whole culture of place making that we are interpreting for the best future of Scotland can be reduced to a long and difficult recovery from two models, the Garden City and the Radiant City, and the countless Levittowns and Pruitt-Igoes[2] that derived from them. Those two models have permeated our urban culture and shaped both our industrial cities and our discipline since their very origins. After so much time and so many realizations, after the environmental challenges posed by global warming and the immense social challenges posed by global urbanization, the shortcomings of such two models are in front of our eyes: they are simply not sustainable anymore. We should retrofit suburbia[3]. We should regenerate futurama[4]. And we should do it now.

There are obstacles in front of us. One may think that such obstacles are very hard to overcome because they are enrooted in complex financial or political problems, but this is not the case. The problem is mainly cultural. And the first thing we can do to move our civilization forward towards better places is to acknowledge that there has been a deep cultural problem, it has mattered a lot, it is still here and it is not going to be removed without effort.

Look around the new 'urban jewels'; give a glance to glamorous architectural journals; listen to what is taught in the best schools of architecture. Generations after generations, we architects still perpetuate the gospel of conventional urbanism in a surreal childish game, where the higher the failure, the greater the honour. Our idea of designing cities is that you should do the job pretty much as if you were designing a building, but just a bit larger. Urban design is still based on the scaling out of our architectural visions. Architects are very young professional figures: in past they were master builders, serving the community by doing the right thing as it had always been done before, which resulted in adopting, preserving and respecting the overall structure of spaces. Even when a different professional figure emerged in the Renaissance and got established in the 18th century, that of the architect scientist, builder and historian who responded to the new needs associated with major specialist buildings, those prominent constructions were conceived as part of the broader urban fabric with which maintained and reinforced the spatial links.

Then, architecture was entirely reconfigured, in a different and even opposite way. We should pay attention to this passage. This passage, at the beginning of the 20th century, is crucial, because architecture changed its status from being a practical art and an experimental science, in the age of the master builders as much as in Palladio's age, to being just a branch of the visual arts in the age of the avant-guards or, as Habraken calls it, the age of "Palladio's children" (Habraken 2005). At this point the dimension of the extraordinary prevailed on the ordinary, which has always been by far the largest portion of our cities, and without even the slightest awareness of that, architects started doing a different job. But the problem is that, in John Habraken's words, "the demands of the everyday environment are vastly different from what is required to create the extraordinary. Nevertheless, the profession's self-image, publications and ways of working still cling to its roots in monumental architecture" (Habraken 2005, p. IX).

The attitude to deal with the ordinary environments of our cities as if they were extraordinary exceptions is the cultural problem of architects-urbanists. This trap has substantially contributed during the 20th century

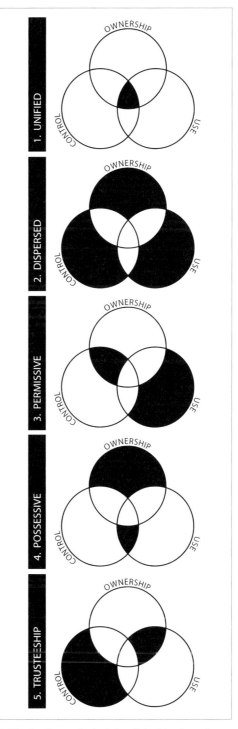

2 The five forms of submission derived by the various combinations of ownership, control and use of spaces by involved parties, redrawn from Akbar 1988, p. 19.

to subvert the very fundamental 'permanent' structures that have been driving the creation and development of our cities throughout time and space, i.e. across history and geography. In parallel, the observation and study of ordinary spaces, i.e. measuring and understanding the form of everyday urban fabrics, developed as a separate discipline named "urban morphology" that is still today a specialism to a great extent detached from the mainstream of practice (Samuels 1990).

Rediscovering the essential properties, the permanent structures of places, being able again to design the contemporary ordinary city: that is at the heart of the challenge. This approach is evidence-based and challenges our mother discipline of architecture to the heart, questioning its very foundations. Apparently, it is a leap into an entirely different scientific domain and begins to delineate the foundations of a different discipline.

2.2. The Oxymoron in Practice: Planning Anti-Planning and Different Forms of Participation

One major characteristic of the different discipline is a focus on self-organization in the formation of urban space. This focus means conceiving the city as the stratification of billions of projects and plans, some large and some small, some collective and some individual, in endless mutual interaction in time. It means seeing what has been negated for too long: that self-organization has nothing to do with chaos; it is in fact a higher level of order. And that most if not all the most lively and successful parts of our cities are in fact those less planned, which means – by definition – more complex. And that the secret of all good cities has always been one specific feature, with which a city can be good or bad depending on many other factors, but it is alive and kicking, and without which a city can just be bad, because it is dead: adaptability. Adaptability, or the structural disposition of spaces to change by welcoming changing needs in time: that is the key.

But if we bring the idea of self-organization from the domains of nature and society, where it has been firstly investigated, to the specific field of urbanism, we find one particular and very profound feature that, if missed, will render our approach too general and eventually blind: self-organization in cities has never been alternative to planning. Quite on the contrary, self-organization in cities has always been the effect of planning: "building the city today could mean the wish to find again, perhaps with different forms, the qualities of proximity, mixture and the unexpected, i.e. a public space accessible to all, a variety of mixed activities, a built-up area that keeps adapting and transforming itself in unplanned neighbourhoods." (Samuels, Panerai, Castex & Depaule 2004, p. 159). Unplanned neighborhoods are the result of adaptations and transformations of formerly planned structures. All major historical centres that we love today and that to our eyes epitomize organic and possibly spontaneous growth are in fact the result of transformation layered in time over structures that had largely been subdivided according to a plan since their very first origin, transformations that – in turn – had often been constituted by the addition and overlapping of single planned developments. It is in fact that kind of planning practice, heavily based on the work of surveyors acting under the commission of landholders (Slater 1988; Conzen 1988), that made it possible for those transformations to occur and keep happening that reshaped a planned fabric into a rich, diverse and seemingly natural built environment.

This is to say that we should escape the flat juxtaposition of planning and self-organization that has so heavily undermined our capacity of innovation in even the most progressive theories of urbanism in the last decades. No one has ever built a significant piece of city in history only by 'spontaneously' adding buildings after buildings without previously parcelling land, setting space for streets and establishing common rules and rights. Admittedly, it was a very fundamental, basic level of planning, but nevertheless it was about setting limits and shaping norms which normally were exactly the right limits and norms, and nothing more than that. So the point, if we are to govern again the realization of human and lively ordinary spaces in our cities, is not necessarily to explore hypothesis of no-planning or radically alternative anti-planning systems: the point is to learn what planning is best fit to set the right spatial structure for future change and adaptation. That is even more true in our times, when we need to achieve by virtue of a conscious and organized effort what once was shared and even unconscious knowledge, i.e. our "spontaneous consciousness" (Caniggia & Maffei 2001, p. 43).

One of the forms that the (fundamentally) anti-planning agenda has increasingly taken in recent times to reaffirm the lost link between communities and their environments is that of "participative planning", meaning the many forms of inclusion of inhabitants or stakeholders in general in a consensus-building decisional process (Innes & Booher 1999). Strengths of this approach are unquestionable, including especially the formation of social and political capitals and the relevance for decision-making of information related with inhabitants' lifeworld, which is key indeed and would otherwise be lost. However, weaknesses of these "collaborative" approaches have been many times outlined as well, both at theoretical and practical level: "I would like to have an evolutionistic trust so to consider acceptable the idea that 'open' urban decision processes will result in better decisions. In a 'Darwinism' of that sort, the free competition of arguments struggling for the same resources (credibility, trust, feasibility …) would come out with the survival of the best decision. Unfortunately I believe firstly that the competition is not free, and secondly that what would survive would just be the strongest argument (in the given situation) which not necessarily brings the system as a whole closer to any improvement". (Porta 2006, p. 113)

What we need to emphasize in the context of this paper is one aspect that is very seldom, if ever, cited: the participative agenda, with all its emphasis on subjects (social actors) that have interests at stake at the moment of creating or regenerating the place, is even more focused than conventional approaches on the design phase, and very rarely takes into account the impacts that designed structures cast on future change. Urban settings do serve generations after generations of human beings in centuries; on the other hand, human needs and values change with people, which means in years and even months. So if the spatial structure is rigid and does not welcome change, it will not accommodate the needs and values of newcomers and therefore will shortly end up in a profoundly anti-human, unsustainable and anti-democratic spatial system, no matter the level of participation that had been originally insufflated into its creation.

That is not to say that processes of participation like charrettes are useless: quite on the contrary, such formal participation is needed to deal with some scales of urban change and some kinds of problems. For example, with some simplification we can associate formal participation to the dimension of the extraordinary: we evidently cannot rely on expensive (in financial and political terms) participative machines to deal with the everyday business of controlling change in everyone's domain. The best feature of formal participation is its capacity to channel information from inhabitants' lifeworld into the decisional arena and that is particularly needed whenever that arena is set at some higher level well off the ground of the ordinary inter-personal, inter-organizational or 'grass-root' gaming. Moreover, experience suggests that formal participation works better where the capitals of public attention, financial resources and political commitment are concentrated on a few relevant decisional processes, as all of those capitals are increasingly insufficient and hard to be regenerated after expenditure. That is the way formal participation should enter, and indeed is entering, the planning system in Scotland.

Our argument is to say that we also need to reactivate the circulation of information between inhabitants and powers through informal processes of participation based not as much on large formal gatherings and structured processes of inclusion as on the daily and direct control of inhabitants over the ordinary modification of their own individual and collective space, at different scales. And for the reasons discussed above, these very traditional processes of informal participation through ordinary change need to be enabled under conditions (including spatial conditions) that must be carefully identified, organized and planned. If such informal processes are not equally embedded in a renovated planning system, the link between planning and the space of the ordinary is destined to fail and so the actual content of democracy in planning to be significantly lowered.

What is the nature of informal participation then? Jamel Akbar (Akbar 1988) helps us in defining this essential problem by focusing on the many forms of control, i.e. who is legitimate to change what in the built environment of the everyday. In describing the differences between the traditional and the modern Muslim city, Akbar analyses what party uses, controls and owns a space. A party is defined as the entity – individual, collective or organizational – that takes decisions. So every space in a city is definable in terms of the relationships of the parties who own, control and use it. Such relationships, or 'forms of submission', are five, as exemplified in the Venn diagrams reported here in figure 2. Now, what turns out is that the form of submission deeply affects crucial dynamics in the formation, maintenance and change of the built environment. For example, when a space is owned, controlled and used by one single party like in the case of a family living in its owned house ('unified' form of submission), maintenance is generally very good, change is gradual and piecemeal and corresponds with the user needs, and the overall environment is socially responsive at the most basic level of society; that was the form of submission that pre-

vailed in the ordinary urban fabric of traditional Muslim cities, but the same applies as a very universal pattern to all traditional cities. At the other extreme, see how a social housing project is owned by a party (the state or the city council), controlled by another (the housing authority) and used by a third (the inhabitants). In this case ('dispersed' form of submission) the environment is very likely to downgrade in terms of maintenance, as inhabitants cannot do repairs or changes without permission and after all they do not have any interest in doing that.

Jamel Akbar's model, that builds on lessons from John Habraken (Habraken 2000), powerfully enlightens the deep nature of processes of change in the space of the ordinary and tells a lot about how we can encourage informal participation in them by orienting the planning process towards one or the other of the various forms of submission and by managing the size of parties involved, which in turn is relevant in understanding what we should borrow from traditional cities in a contemporary version of plot-based urbanism. It is important to understand in fact that the space of self-organization so typically supported by pre-modern urban fabrics will never come back on its own under present day's conditions, which in fact typically inhibit it or, in other words, 'kill it in the cradle'. If we want self-organization to start up and take on in cities, we must plan them in a specific manner with that objective in mind. And here we see the programme of the different discipline: we must explore the spatial, social, financial and political structures that will enable and feed once again processes of self-organization and informal participation in contemporary cities.

We should not underestimate the magnitude of the challenge: it is that far more subtle process that we should reinforce and reanimate in a new contemporary – but timeless in nature – form of city planning. Therefore, to be true, we are not speaking of urban design or planning anymore: we are speaking of this different discipline, under a different name, that of urban seeding. This term resounds Christopher Alexander's words:

"This quality in buildings and in towns cannot be made, but only generated, indirectly, by the ordinary actions of the people, just as a flower cannot be made, but only generated from the seed." (Alexander 1980). However, we should not, equally, overestimate this challenge. The relevant part of change, the heart of the magic of cities, is the one that takes place after the initial conception and construction of spaces, informally, through time, spanning across generations, and that never ends. This is the part that the new discipline should study, understand, enable and preserve under present conditions. So the process that the new discipline must manage differently is as much the process of spaces' creation, as that of spaces' control and change after the creation phase. Provided that the 'right' structuring principles are in place, a street or a neighbourhood can well be created throughout processes of many different kinds, including several very conventional top-down ones, and still initiate a local history of success that is informally democratic for future generations of inhabitants and users. Conversely, if the right principles are forgotten and left behind, even the most radically community-oriented and inclusive processes of design may end up in schemes informed by the highest rigidity which therefore are inherently non-democratic, in that they do not allow future generations to control and change their spaces (and indeed we have plenty of examples of that). So what is really important for the different discipline is, much more than devising and implementing the right process, devising the right principles and understanding how these can inform a variegated set of processes.

Once the fundamental relevance of this informal process is definitely acknowledged, we cannot but re-tune the scope of our work as city planners and designers. Our mission should neither be to create identity, or beauty, or to determine (social, economic) success by design, nor to shape the process that by itself will inject beauty or democracy in our plans, being them finalized to a fixed state like in conventional or participative plans or to a continuously operating set of norms like in more suggestive generative approaches. Our mission as urban designers is, in fact, to ensure the minimal spatial conditions (right principles) for informal adaptation to start, expand and continue in time. Understanding which are those conditions, and which form they may conveniently take in practice under local financial and legal burdens, should be clearly set as our professional duty as scientists, scholars and practitioners.

Driven by this mission, and within this new framework, what we should do in practice is clear and, to some extent, relatively easily to approach, as it no longer implies penetrating into an unknown societal, political and disciplinary territory. We should look back to our planning tradition with a new question in mind: what is the technical content of those plans that have demonstrated the capacity to accommodate, enhance, and maintain in time a sufficient level of informal participation? And in particular: what was designed and what was left undefined? And finally: what can we learn from them that can be successfully applied under present conditions for the regeneration of today's cities? In other words, we should de-emphasize the importance of a planning intervention as a specific act of creation, and stress it being the starting point of a local history whose success is greater where the change is not dictated by the plan itself but achieved through time. The different discipline starts with a focus on all processes of post-design, in explicit contrast to the contemporary obsession with the design phase that permeates architecture and urban design alike.

We do not know what this different discipline, which we provisionally name urban seeding, is going to be in detail. If its construction is going to happen, it will not happen as a genial revelation from one person or group but as a gradual collective construction led by an increasing level of consciousness. We know, however, several of its key aspects that we are searching for. Whatever this new discipline will be, it will have to do with:

– Evidence-based solutions, as opposed to design-based solutions.
– An emphasis on the dimension of the ordinary and a science of the common sense, as opposed to the dimension of the extraordinary and a rhetoric of the stunning.
– A major interest in post-design, i.e. in spatial change and evolution, as opposed to a notion of the intangibility of the work-of-art.
– A priority interest in processes of informal participation, as complementary to formal processes of collaborative planning.
– A structural approach that emphasises what is recurrent in space and time (within certain spatial and temporal domains), as opposed to the analytical approach that privileges what is different in space and time.
– A stylistic neutral attitude, as opposed to style-led urbanism.

3. PLOT-BASED URBANISM

Plot-based urbanism is the set of spatial principles conducive to urban spaces that are adaptable over time and therefore fit the agenda of urban seeding. These principles are spatial in nature, which means that they are not necessarily related with any particular kind of planning process: on the contrary, every process that embeds these principles is conducive to adaptable spaces.

Plot-based urbanism owes its denomination to the acknowledgment of the fundamental importance of the plot in the spatial structure of ordinary urban fabrics. How the plot is shaped, its size and geometry, its relationship with the street and the street hierarchy, how it forms up street fronts and eventually urban blocks, how all this informs human activities and urban functions, and finally how the plot finds a correspondence with property, usage and control, all that is fundamentally the matter of plot-based urbanism. However, plot-based urbanism doesn't mean that eve-

rything that is made of plots is fine. Plot-based urbanism is a specific kind of spatial structure made of a certain kind of plots, juxtaposed and mixed in a certain way, establishing a certain kind of relationship with the streets they front, etc. Eventually, issues of density and compactness are inherently part of the question. Ultimately, plot-based urbanism is place making made time-conscious.

A few key concepts ought to be introduced at this point: PLOT, STREET, CENTRALITY, STREET FRONT and BLOCK as well as their changed fortune in history as elements constituting the fabric of our places.

Plot: A plot is a fenced portion of land that is entirely accessible from the public space. Though plot and property may coincide, and very often do, what defines a plot is accessibility, not property. A result of this definition is that large properties may be split into small plots without necessarily subdividing the property of the land. In all such cases, plots are to be interpreted as the ultimate units of development.

Street: A street is a mostly open space that is publicly accessed and establishes a functional, visual and spatial link with private domains, i.e. plots, by which it is defined. Cities exist and evolve across centuries, through endless changes of different magnitude happening at different pace. Streets tend to be the most permanent elements of all, imposing conditions to the fabric that sits on them. Streets are highly loaded with character and changing in type, meaning and value whilst penetrating the city. When allowed, they establish a functional and formal relationship with such fabric in terms of fundamental factors like density, land use, size and geometry and accessibility of plots. Such relationships are mainly the product of the evolution of the fabric in time, being selected according to local conditions including environmental, cultural, technical and financial. The key factor that constitutes the link between street and plots is centrality.

Centrality: Centrality is here intended as a particular character attached to streets by their geometry (i.e. length) and topology (i.e. the way they are connected to each other). Work conducted in UDSU (Porta, Crucitti & Latora 2006) as well as elsewhere (Hillier & Hanson 1984; Hillier 1996) has led to mapping and modelling street centrality in a reliable and scientifically grounded way. Subsequent work is studying the formal relationships between streets and frontages to understand patterns of change of the latter in relation to change in the former. Studies in this line of research are beginning to raise evidence on these key relationship and, though there is a long way to go before these factors are sufficiently understood in detail, research is nonetheless firmly settled in its discipline, i.e. urban morphology, and therefore likely to develop relatively quickly.

Street Front: Street Fronts are the formation of plots facing on a street. They are the key components of urban blocks, yet their relation to streets is, in history, more direct and important. If a street front can adapt to a street's character over time it makes it more versatile; if on the other hand it is linked to a whole block, its capacity to change and adapt is restricted, its lifespan shortened, with implications on character and quality of life. Street fronts are made of plots; and yet again, plots have followed in time markets and density adapting in size to the nature of the street, which eventually is heavily influenced by its centrality.

Block: An urban block is a mainly built-up urban area defined on its borders bystreets, whose components are street fronts. We intend the urban block as a complex rather than a uniform element. Its character may vary a lot on each street front depending on the type of streets it faces upon. An ordinary urban block exhibits four street fronts, because it normally sits on four streets. Because streets generally possess different importance (main, local, secondary …) depending on their centrality, the street fronts constituting an urban block reflect such diversity. This is due, again, by the evolutionary character of the ordinary urban fabric: its formation is led by streets developing in time from the most to the less central, a process which is accompanied by the subdivision of adjacent land in plots and therefore the constructions of street fronts. Urban blocks are the result of this stepped process, not its constituent unit: they are formed by the completion of this cycle of formation when it reaches the point where four streets close up in a loop and their street fronts get consequently developed. Planning strategies, especially those related with coding, should acknowledge this peculiar process by assuming that the unit of analysis and coding is the street front, rather than the block.

This is indeed nothing new. The 'spontaneous' growth of cities has always proceeded by parcelling and then building up the two fronts of streets, starting from the most central ones, where the city originated, and then generating and filling up the less central in time (see below Ch. 3.2: "400-MTS RULE"). According to Caniggia and Maffei: "However, it is wise to note especially the essential consequence of tracing connecting routes: the final achievement of the block concept as the most eye catching and widely used module of the urban aggregate. In a certain sense, it is also the most questionable, because it will soon be clear from the genesis reconstructed through route typology that blocks are progressively determined by the coordination of several pertinent strips of each route and that each pertinent strip is definitely more cohesive and consistent with the reciprocal one, inherent to the route itself, than those re-emerged in the block. This arises because of the contemporaneousness of buildings along opposite sides of the same route and due to these sides being constantly subject to progressive, similar changes during the course of their history." (Caniggia and Maffei 2001, p. 133)

This point, which might seem somehow not essential, is in fact one of the most profound features of traditional urbanism. If taken seriously, it makes the difference between contemporary pseudo-traditionalism, a widely practiced character even in the most fashionable place-making realizations of our days, and a different plot-based discipline: "Nevertheless the fact of having brought the block to the foreground has had

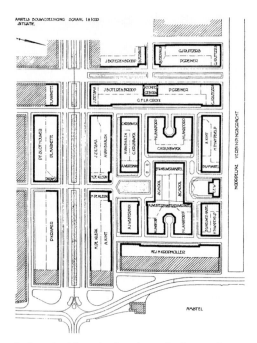

3 An extract from the Amstel area development in Amsterdam, an implementation of 1917 Amsterdam-Zuid Plan designed by Berlage. The figure shows the names of the architects in charge for the design of street fronts: the same names appear on both sides of the streets (Samuels, Panerai, Castex & Depaule 2004, p. 85).

some perverse effects. It has brought the careless reader or the hurried designer to transform the issue into a caricature: city = block or modernity = single building. The new neighbourhoods of the new towns or modest urban renovation were thus filled with pseudo-blocks, which are but the urbanistic rendering of a valueless postmodern formalism. This has brought us to develop the initial conclusion insisting on the importance of the subdivision of plots and of the status of spaces and of developing a reflective attitude towards the projects." (Samuels, Panerai, Castex & Depaule 2004)

Interesting enough, the same happened in the early years of the planning profession, too, in an age when still the traditional formation of cities was 'unconsciously' part of the planners' mindset. We allege [3] the example of development in Amsterdam after the second version of the Zuid Plan elaborated by Hendrik

Petrus Berlage in 1917. In this case the municipality commissioned to the same architect both fronts of one street, rather than the four fronts of one block. The result is the emergence of an overall consistency of building materials and language still in presence of a great variety of specific solutions where the same block was ultimately designed by different architects. Research on 20 small Scottish towns has shown the evolution of urban blocks through transitions from traditional to modern and from modern to post-modern (Hart, Hooi, Romice & Porta 2010). In the first transition, for many well documented reasons (the car being the most influential), blocks expanded in size, decreased in functional complexity, lost front definition and became fairly homogeneous in structure, a pattern that is certainly not limited to Scotland but in fact is very general across at least the Western world (Samuels, Panerai, Castex & Depaule 2004). The consequences of this change have been immense: block size impacted on access and movement, uniformity of functions and zoning, while lack of front definition largely affected the character of places. Moreover, the overall drop in density had been of sufficient magnitude to change forever the destiny of our cities. These structural changes had severe social repercussions: the separation of users and uses as well as the death of the street as a place for public life. In the second transition (modern to post-modern which has then led to the now widely practice of place making), a lot changed to address the consequences of this block expansion on the form and performance of the city; nevertheless the size of blocks themselves remains fairly unchanged. The street is correctly perceived as the generator of life, and street layouts are amended, designed and implemented to encourage activity to take place. Architecture is scaled down to the people but, crucially, the block is still perceived as the design unit of the urban realm, like for example in the IBA experience in Berlin 1987 (Kleihues 1987). At the heart of plot-based urbanism is the understanding that streets and street fronts require diversity and adaptability to support urban life; in design terms this implies, very simply, smaller units. The modernist/place-making block is still unitary in its overall conception and execution because it is conceived as the unit. The traditional city block was smaller and made of aggregations of smaller units, the plots. Plots have a direct relation to the street, with a profound impact on diversity and character, but also to the number of entrances to the block, with impact on activity within the block. Moreover, plots are independent, with impact on the diversity of the block, and guarantee that such diversity reflects the streets on which the block sits, impacting on its responsiveness to city life.

Because a more definitive and clear definition of what plot-based urbanism is in practice is matter of ongoing research, some past and current examples might help tracing the way forward.

3.1. Cases

Case 1

Middle Age, Firenze: Planning the Urban Expansion, 1250–1350
Author: Gian Luigi Maffei

Between 1250 and 1350 the significant growth in population before the Great Plague (1348) brought the number of residents in Florence to about 100,000 people. The urban developments that sheltered this additional population were built in two successive phases, first at Oltrarno in 1259 and then in general in 1280/1333; these were then surrounded by a new urban wall erected outside the earlier one (constructed in 1173/1175). [4]

These areas were owned by conventual orders, hospitals and arts and crafts guilds, which therefore became the promoters of allotments which constituted the new urban developments. Allotments, like the San Frediano estate which is reported below in figure 4, were usually designed along existing streets and property lines: the "matrix routes" were pre-existent routes which were built up in the first place, then orthogonal streets were built and finally the urban block was closed by a fourth path. The link between path and plot is still clearly legible looking at the "pertinent fringe areas" of each front. Patterns of a different kind were always due to cadastral constraints.

The evolution of the housing type took the form of a passage from single to multi-family buildings and then, with the successive merging of three to four adjacent plots to realize buildings with two flats per storey. These transformations and the higher or lower density of medieval urban fabrics are a consequence of the different nodal quality of local places, either original or induced by the evolution of fabric itself in time. Plots were generally sized with fronts of 8/9 Florentine Arms (the Florentine Arm was equal to 0.58 cm) and depths of 30/40/50 arms depending on the degree of centrality of the plot's location. Such plots corresponded to the inner needs of the most popular building type of the times, the row house. Plots were rented under condition that the construction of the building was started by a certain agreed deadline and upon the payment of an annual rent. It often happened that the tenant could not pay the rent and the

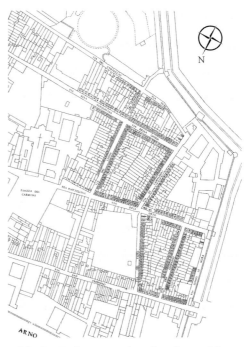

4 The San Frediano estate, located southwest of the Arno River. The estate was planned as an urban development between mid-13th and mid-14th centuries by the monastic order of Camaldoli that was settled in the adjacent Carmine Monastery. In this cadastral drawing houses are numbered that were owned by the order still in the 17th century (Canniggia and Maffei 2001).

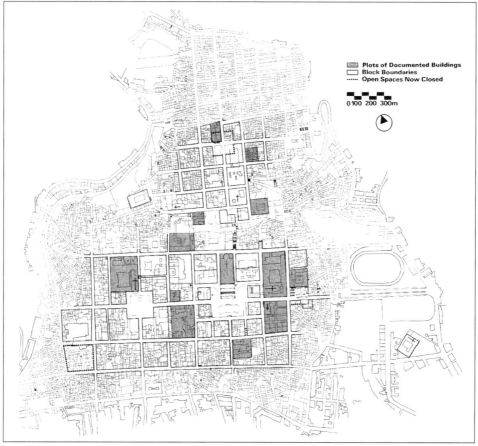

5 View of Noto from the South and plan of Noto in 1712.

building returned to the landlord: as a result, subjects that initially played as just landlords became rapidly relevant real estate operators.

Case 2
Baroque Age, Noto: Planning the New City after the 1693 Earthquake
Author: Peter Russell

In 1693 the Sicilian town of Noto was destroyed by "an earthquake so horrible and ghastly that the soil undulated like the waves of a stormy sea, and the mountains danced as if drunk, and the city collapsed in one miserable moment killing more than a thousand people." (Tobriner 1982) The destroyed town was abandoned, left to become a city of ruins, Noto Antica. The new town of Noto was settled seven kilometres away on the summit of the Meti, a small mountain near the coast. From 1693 to 1702 the success of the move from the site of Noto Antica to that of Noto Nuova was not certain.

In an effort to ensure the settlement of the new city on the Meti summit, the nobility deeded land to "anyone who needed it" (Tobriner 1982, p. 46). Where a vacant building plot existed in the city the nobility would give the land to a suitable settler, who would lose ownership of the plot if they failed to build and develop the plot. Building plots were given to the clergy and aristocracy, those who could afford to invest in building. The selection of the building site for Noto served their interests and desires for the opportunity to build a new provincial centre in the 17th and 18th century aesthetic, as much as any practical function. In the mid-18th century Noto was recovering slowly, with a population half that of the pre-earthquake Noto Antica.

The city developed both on the summit and the slope of the Meti, and had two resulting non-aligned street grids. [5] The building plots also developed in a duplicitous manner, with buildings fronting main roads and the sloping grid having a very regular pattern following the street, and buildings on the interior of the block and at the city periphery having a seemingly random pattern. The heavily coordinated and patterned portions of the city were deeded to and developed by the aristocracy and the clergy, producing an urban landscape in the aesthetic they desired when they elected to relocate the city. The wide streets and defined piazzas were lost entirely at the city's perimeter, where the peasant class developed the land in a more ad hoc manner responding to the topography and ultimately developing a more medieval pattern. The city divided, presents itself as both a Baroque city in its centre and a medieval city at the fringe.

Building plots of Noto are carefully measured around the central part of the city, and in both the grid of the summit and that of the slope. Plots and block interiors of the urban periphery are more random and organic, emerging more gradually, necessitating winding, narrow alleys. Exterior plots developed first, subsidised by the aristocracy and clergy, interior plots developed slowly, as a requirement of increasing population. Blocks that were laid out for dwellings were planned and built as perimeter blocks with gardens and a small lane traversing the block. A growing population led to these gardens being developed into residential units, and smaller dwellings, blocking the through lane forming an interior courtyard, and a network of smaller lanes.

This pattern of development results in Noto exhibiting a fractured urban form. The two misaligned grids of the city are composed of perimeter blocks, which in all but the most sacred locations were long ago subdivided into smaller plots and infilled with smaller buildings. Outer parts of the city exhibit an even higher level of density resulting in smaller plots, which completely cover blocks that all but disregard the grid pattern, traversed several times by narrow alleys and lanes in the style of Noto Antica.

The subdivision of plots and the breakdown of the Baroque grid (on the block interiors) furthered the medieval nature of Noto. The plot structure in Noto has shown little physical evolution in over 250 years since the infill of its original perimeter blocks. This demonstrates the exceptional degree of adaptability embedded in the plots and blocks comprising the urban structure of Noto. The functional evolution of Noto's plots further demonstrates the adaptable nature of the urban framework. Monumental buildings in the centre of Noto have evolved as users demands

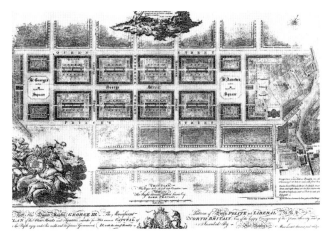

6 James Craig's original plan of Edinburgh's New Town, 1767.

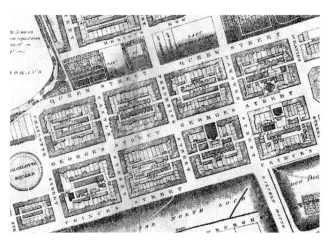

8 Ainslie's map of Edinburgh, 1804.

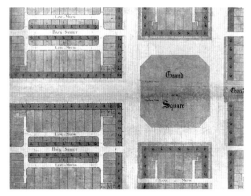

7 Excerpt from James Craig's feu plan, 1767.

evolved from ecclesiastical to civic to educational uses. The evolution and adaptability of the plots and architecture and their interaction with the Baroque era grid and medieval style framework of lanes has allowed Noto to escape the modernisation effects so apparent in other 18th century cities.

Case 3

Enlightenment Age, Edinburgh: The First New Town, 1767–1807

Authors: David Howell, Gillian Black

Edinburgh's Town Council, in the mid-17th century, demonstrated a grand, civic example of historical plot-based development which many lessons can still be learned from today. In acquiring land to the north of the existing town core, a substantially-scaled expansion was initiated with the separating valley (contained the Nor Loch) drained and bridged, a process that took over a decade, before the decision was made to prepare a plan for the development of the New Town. The intention was that this expansion should be an aristocratic classically-designed residential area to house the town's upper classes whilst the grand streets were also to contain smaller spaces for the serving classes.

A competition was set in 1766 to produce a plan for the laying out of this prestigious new development, which was subsequently won by the 21 year-old James Craig, who created a classically inspired plan to support social hierarchy and civic grandeur through its combination of grand streets, mews lanes and axial linking of squares, churches and views. [6] Craig developed the detailed feu plan along with a sewer plan which provided comfort to potential purchasers of plots that the land would be serviced properly.

The rectangular, gridiron plan centred on George Street, which ran along the topographical ridge, with the two main squares (and associated civic building plots) at either end and was bound by Queen Street to the north and Princes Street to the south. The feu plan [7] divided the eight main "perimeter and mews" blocks into plots with dimensions reflecting their position in the street (and associated social) hierarchy – the detail of the building footprints and private gardens were clearly detailed alongside letters denoting feu values. The values against the plots were driven by their street hierarchy position, the building height limit (four-storey on main streets and two-storey in mews lanes) as well as their views – whether south towards the rocky outcrop of the mediaeval town core, or north towards the uninterrupted views towards Fife ([8] shows the contrast in plot and street arrangement between old and new towns).

The strong design was of course achievable due to the land ownership control of the Town Council whilst the ability to fund the substantial infrastructure works was due to a period of wealthy prosperity based on Edinburgh's financial industry. This civic strength allowed for such an ambitious plan and the wealth of the individuals purchasing plots in the New Town and their feu duty payments to the town also supported this growth. The development of the plots themselves (over a period of 40 years from 1767) was undertaken by a range of builders and wealthy individuals who utilised their architects to meet the standards and design required of the feu plan – a plan which was amended over time to allow for a wider range of plots to accommodate professionals and institutions as well as the aristocracy.

The streets were feued in phases to ensure completion of blocks and in the Charlotte Square designed by Robert Adam, a payment incentive was made to the first feuar to roof their house first, thus ensuring swift plot completions. Over time, the plots accommodated a greater extent of commercial uses and the in-built adaptability of the New Town design and its ability to sustain change has been demonstrated by its 200 year successful transition from upper-class residential suburb to mixed-use civic core.

Case 4

Industrial Age, Glasgow: Suburbanization at Hyndland, 1897–1910
Authors: Wolfgang Sonne, David Howell, Gillian Black

The case of Glasgow, "the tenement city" par excellence (Reed 1993; Cockburn 1925), can be used to highlight the fact that the perimeter block, subdivided into house units, was firmly rooted in urban design of the 18th century. Glasgow's first new town plan from 1782 by James Barry showed a pattern of large residential perimeter blocks around George Square, which was then repeated within the Blythswood new town (Arneil-Walker 1993). During the 19th century, the pattern of rectangular tenement blocks, usually four storeys high and containing shops on the ground

1870 Post Office Directory Map of Glasgow's West End

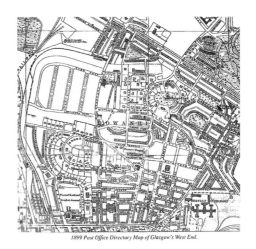

1899 Post Office Directory Map of Glasgow's West End.

9 Hyndland estate in the context of adjoining estate development and railway infrastructure.

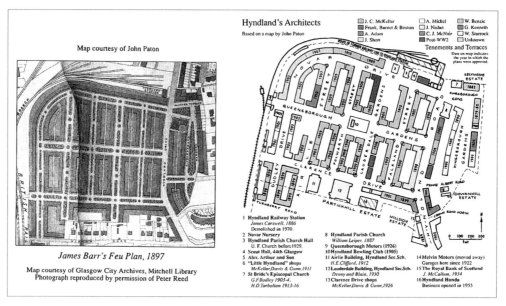

Map courtesy of John Paton

James Barr's Feu Plan, 1897

Map courtesy of Glasgow City Archives, Mitchell Library
Photograph reproduced by permission of Peter Reed

Hyndland's Architects
Based on a map by John Paton

□ J. C. McKellar   □ A. Mickel   ■ W. Benzie
■ Frank, Burnet & Boston   ■ J. Nisbet   ■ G. Kenneth
■ A. Adam   ■ C. J. McNair   ■ W. Sturrock
■ J. Short   ■ Post-WW2   □ Unknown

Tenements and Terraces
Date on map indicates
the year in which the
plans were approved.

1 Hyndland Railway Station
   James Carswell, 1886
   Demolished in 1970.
2 Novar Nursery
3 Hyndland Parish Church Hall
   U. F. Church before 1929.
4 Scout Hall, 44th Glasgow
5 Alex. Arthur and Son
6 "Little Hyndland" shops
   McKellar,Davis & Gunn,1911
7 St Bride's Episcopal Church
   *G.F.Bodley 1903-4,
   H.O.Tarbolton 1913-16*
8 Hyndland Parish Church
   William Leiper, 1887
9 Queensborough Motors (1926)
10 Hyndland Bowling Club (1905)
11 Airlie Building, Hyndland Sec.Sch.
   H.E.Clifford, 1912
12 Lauderdale Building, Hyndland Sec.Sch.
   Denny and Blain, 1930
13 Clarence Drive shops
   McKellar,Davis & Gunn,1926
14 Melvin Motors (moved away)
   Garages here since 1922
15 The Royal Bank of Scotland
   J. McCallum, 1934
16 Hyndland Honda
   Business opened in 1955

10 Feu plan for Hyndland, 1897, and architect/builder block variety.

floor towards major streets, was used for both middle-class and workers' dwellings (Worsdall 1979). As legislation did not allow for internal wings, all of these blocks were characterised by large internal courtyards which in most cases had been planted. In the working class neighbourhoods, these blocks were designed as units enclosed on all sides, the most uniform areas being Hutchesontown, Govanhill and Dennistoun, all developed during the 1870s and 1880s. In the middle-class neighbourhoods, the block was often subdivided by a lane, thus combining the socially higher model of the terrace with the lower model of the tenement block. Exemplary areas include Woodlands and Hyndland, with the latter being built according to James Barr's plan between 1897 and 1910 as a wealthy Edwardian tenement quarter with most of the buildings by John Campbell McKellar, including a central green square, tree lined streets and green courts (Laird 1997). Even if all these blocks had been planned as area developments, each block had been structured by town house units, each having its own entrance. Thus each block was potentially subdivided into plots. In Glasgow the tenement block with a large courtyard followed a long-lasting tradition and helped to create

a city with dwelling quarters which were both extremely urban and pleasant, allowing for a variety of dwellers and uses and nevertheless creating a unique urban harmony.

The Hyndland estate in Glasgow's West End was developed by several builders and a variety of architects, largely between 1897 and 1910. The land was situated on the western periphery of the city, adjacent the estates of Dowanhill, Kelvinside and Partickhill, which had been subject of speculative development, mainly in the form of grand terraces and villas to house the growing middle classes on the back of Glasgow's industrial growth. [9] The Hyndland land had been acquired in 1876 but development was delayed by an economic recession and it was not until the mid-1890s that plans were revisited, supported by public transit improvements in the form of horse-drawn trams (developing into electric trams by 1907) and a passenger rail service to the area (introduced via a new spur from the main line in 1886 when very few buildings existed in the area). The landowner instigated a feu plan for the area, completed by James Barr in 1897 [10], which was based on prevailing market conditions to provide middle-class apartments as a more affordable alternative to the terraces of Great Western Road to the north. The plan divided the land (west of Hyndland Road) into a grid with regular blocks bound by one long perimeter block to the west and north (acting as barrier to the rail lines) with dividing streets containing 'pleasure gardens'.

The symmetrical layout design was based on the tenement footprint and adjustments to the plan allowed for a variety of supporting amenities such as small parks, a bowling green (acting as a visual focus within the fairly rigid block structure), two rows of single-storey shop units on main roads along with plots for schools, churches and community buildings.

Common design elements controlled by feu conditions included a four-storey building limit, use of red sandstone and slate roofs. The feued land was acquired by a builder on the basis of the conditions of the feu plan, who then sold on plots to other builders and associated architects. In many cases, completed tenements were sold on to a property company whose business focused on renting the individual flats and acting as property factor to recover maintenance fees and rental payments. In other cases flats were let directly by the builders and it was not until after the First World War that sales became the norm.

Land acquisition and development was made possible through investment by shareholders in a new development company, who were willing to take a longer-term view through dividends based on a mix of selling completed blocks or individual lets.

The structure and design of Hyndland has largely been retained in the 100 years since its completion with only a handful of infill developments. [11] The initial plan effectively mirrors a form of transit-oriented, plot-based development which exploited the potential of rail and tram connections in a (then) suburban periphery location. The high-density form of the tenement was utilised to meet a demand for affordable middle-class accommodation with amenities and services located on primary streets. The long-term involvement of the developer through property management and an emphasis on rental not individual ownership ensured the enduring quality of the area, augmented by title conditions which other builders had to conform to which delivered the desired quality of product. Design variety was achieved through a variety of architects and builders and adaptability was achievable in theory through the blocks being divided into plots which each tenement was developed on, although it could equally have been townhouses should the market have desired.

Case 5

Post-Industrial Age, Amsterdam: Regeneration of Java Island, 1991/2000
Author: Sjoerd Soeters

Java Island is a narrow peninsula (130 metres wide and 1200 metres long) in Amsterdam's Eastern Harbour District which was built in 1900 for the arrival of large ocean going ships. When the port activities shifted westwards, this harbour became gradually redundant and Amsterdam decided to transform the Eastern Harbour District into a residential area.

The city's planning department formulated in 1990 an overall vision for the entire district and directed the development. Various urban designers and supervisors were engaged to work up the schemes for the individual peninsulas.

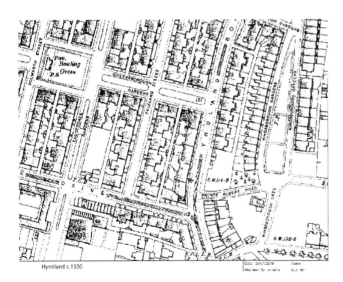

11 An early plan (approx. 1930) detailing the Hyndland subdivision at the eastern fringe of the development.

12 The structure of narrow and deep 'gothic' plots, reminiscent of the ancient structure of the historic city centre, is clearly visible in this shot of the side canals waterfront in Java Island, Amsterdam.

For Java Island, the city's planning department carried out a preliminary study, formulated the development brief and produced a model plan. This development brief stipulated, among other things, that the development was to be situated parallel to the quays in order to exploit the view over the IJ. Because there was no space on the narrow island for a wide central road, car traffic had to be routed via the north quay. Bicycle traffic was to be routed over a cycle path through the sheltered, less windy central area. Another important part of the development brief was the so-called *Woonatlas*, the Atlas of Dwelling, produced by the city of Amsterdam, which described concepts of living. Starting point for this atlas was the observation that the combination of building for the housing market and the growing differentiation of locations and life styles needed new concepts of living: different people, different wishes. This resulted in a list of different types of dwellings, in which the focal point was the number of occupants and the degree of collectivity or individuality.

At this point, the city's planning department contracted four developers and housing corporations, who could also take part in the development of the urban plan, under the condition that they contribute towards the costs. They were also asked to give input from their point of view as developers regarding the feasibility of the whole project.

Three architectural offices were then invited to draw up a scheme based on this: Geurst and Schultze, Sjoerd Soeters and Rudy Uytenhaak. The scheme by Sjoerd Soeters was chosen to be realized, with additions from Uytenhaak and the city's planning department.

The island is partitioned by creating four lateral canals. On these narrow lateral canals are individual canal houses. The apartment buildings along the quays are relatively small and of a size that fits in well with the large dimensions of the island and the water

13 An aerial view of the Java Island in Amsterdam.

14 A street front in Rajkot, India, built through a Town Planning Scheme process. The plot-based structure coupled with a disjointed development leads to a great variety of architectural solutions that nevertheless still obey to an overall framework; a dynamic similar to that observed in the Java Island case.

yet keeps the human scale in mind. The buildings are 27 metres wide and divided into five naves of 5.4 metres. Each building contains approximately 20 dwellings and is, based upon the *Woonatlas*, meant for different target groups: Work/Hobby, Families, Low Budget and Representative. All these different units were then randomly divided over the island and designed by different architects. Within this structure, each building has its own programme of functions, access and design.

In order to realise a large degree of unity and a great deal of variation and alternation within the continuity of the quay buildings, different types of plans were required, as well as a number of architectural rules, in order to prevent a 'design war'. "The variety of each is dominated by the harmony of the whole", was the slogan with which plasticity in the facades is restored to the thickness of the house front itself. Unity of materials (everything brick) and colour (all frames white) was prescribed and variety in the heights of the windowsills and the buildings was required. The windows had to be designed in series and rhythms, the facades not frontal but in perspective.

The building unit on the quays, buildings that are 27 metres wide, are present on the canals in miniature form: canal houses that differ in height, form, colour and material, but are nonetheless part of a series in which unity is sought. [12] Therefore the overall subdivision of the entire area, which originally was one single very large property, into a number of much smaller units of development or plots, each of which then subjected to separate processes involving different stakeholders, is at the heart of the success of the plan. [13]

Case 6

Post-Industrial Age, Rajkot: The Town Planning Scheme Model
Author: Bakulesh Rupani

Since 1914 India's planning process is based on a so-called Town Planning Scheme (TPS) model, which is successfully implemented and has proven able to achieve the desired built form on plots.

The TPS is principally a self-sustainable partnership project set by landowners of a development area, where the authority plays the role of facilitator. The land, which typically belongs to different owners, is brought in to a pool (original plot), redefined in form of master plan by the authority (final plot) and then redistributed to landowners with 25 to 30 per cent cutting as a pay back against infrastructures being made available at door step. The TPS model also provides land for urban poor and public purposes. The authority, initially, pays all the costs for infrastructure and then recovers from the sales of land achieved from cuttings as well as betterment charges levied upon landowners.

TPS is therefore a comprehensive plan of land with plots shaped for different purposes like residential, commercial, institutional etc., which makes provision for all necessary infrastructure and civic amenities. It is a tool to make scarce land in the urban areas available for public purposes. It also facilitates major BOT based projects, generating finance by way of auction of commercial plots. [14]

TPSs are prepared under The Gujarat Town Planning and Urban Development Act, 1976. TPSs are developed in three stages: (i) Draft Scheme; (ii) Preliminary Scheme; (iii) Final Scheme. The Draft TPS is prepared by the local authority under the Act. The Government approves and then appoints a Town Planning Officer to finalize the Preliminary and Final TPSs. The Preliminary TPS contains details about the physical part of the scheme while the final layout contains details about the financial part.

Social infrastructure, commercial activities, garden, open spaces are planned and disposed in a proximity structure in any TPS, which leads to neighbourhood planning. A variety of housing types and a provision of plots for housing which mixes social as well as economic classes lead to well integrated and socially cohesive developments.

The financial burden for development is not passed on to anyone's shoulders. The authority gets land for development and stakeholders get unearned increment for their land that leads to economic sustainability. A hierarchy of roads where commercial and institutional uses are located on main roads while inner roads are for residential and other enhance the logistic efficiency. The option of walking, biking, and using public transit, in addition to driving, reduces traffic congestion and contributes to environmental efficiency. Garden, parks, community hall, school, library, hospital, all available in the vicinity, enhance public participation, and this in turn leads to higher moral values in society.

In conclusion, the final plot is the end product in any TPS. Regulations are framed regarding features like type of development, access to the plot, abutting road width, size of plot, permissible built-up volume, while other are pertaining to the final plot only. Hence a plot is the basic unit and all the plots together define the urban form of the city.

3.2. Learning from Cases: Principles of Adaptable and Democratic Spaces

The cases show how, in different places and in different eras, urban fabric has been planned and then successfully evolved in seemingly organic shapes, generating memorable environments inhabited and loved by generations. Whilst not consciously planned for change, they had been planned in such a way that allowed change to happen at many scales without any central coordination, and have continued to happen restlessly up to our days involving individuals, groups and organizations alike in making decisions directly and informally.

Luckily, an increasing number of recent initiatives show the same can happen today, under the most different financial, political and demographic conditions; cases like the Java Island in Amsterdam, The Netherlands, and the TPSs in Rajkot, India, for all their differences, illuminate this possibility at least with reference to some of their specific aspects.

Learning from cases, we can add a few organizing principles to the list of components already identified (PLOT, STREET, CENTRALITY, STREET FRONT, BLOCK). We do so by looking at the most evident similarities among these cases: because of their permanence across time and space, these principles emerge as key factors in the formation of plot-based urban fabrics.

Small Plots: Small plots are essential. They are ubiquitously present across all cases allowing a vital city to emerge and grow at any time in history. Of course plots can and must vary in size and geometry, but they can't exceed either way beyond a certain limit. Too large plots may be fit to host certain special functions in a city (indeed they are really necessary in very few cases) but they are lethal to ordinary urban spaces: because they don't afford change in time, they are conducive to rigid patterns of use that are inappropriate for ordinary uses. Small plots, however, do not necessarily mean small properties. Large properties can (and should) be subdivided in many small plots in order to favor flexibility of uses, diversity and efficient forms of submission, conducive to disjointed development.

Plot-Street Relationship: The essential engine of urban fabric evolution in time is the relationship that links plots and streets. In practice this means three fundamental things.

First: a development should never be designed block by block, but rather street front by street front. As a consequence, guiding parameters (i.e. codes) should be about setting conditions of street fronts, not of blocks. Street fronts hence should be taken as the coding units of a new generation of form-based codes Second: density, size, geometry and uses of a plot are largely dependent on street centrality. Therefore, understanding and managing street centrality is key, while planning a city, to drive its informal evolution. Third: wherever density grows beyond the minimal threshold, say around 20–30 units per hectare (gross),

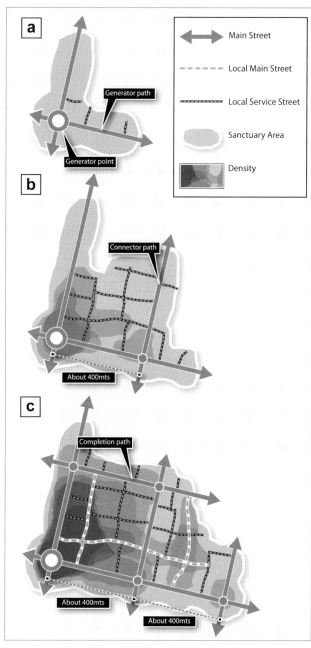

Main Street

Local Main Street

Local Service Street

Sanctuary Area

Density

15 *The '400 meters rule' as emerging from the process of evolution of cities during cycles of expansion. Thick red solid lines are main streets; dashed orange lines are local main streets; thin dotted yellow lines are local service streets. Grades of brown express levels of building density. In this model, Main Streets enclose mostly residential urban districts named Sanctuary Areas: such areas are made of blocks which are formed in time by the densification of built fronts along Local Streets (Mehaffy, Porta, Rofè & Salingaros 2010).*

street fronts are built directly on street without significant setbacks. That leads to the formation in time of perimeter blocks, which are the constituent part of any dense, compact urban fabric. Blocks are nevertheless to be intended as functionally and formally linked aggregation of street fronts. The character of the link between plots and streets is place-specific and must be investigated locally, but the link in itself is essential everywhere.

400-Meters Rule: The 400-meters rule is an organizational model of evolving cities first presented in 2009 at CNU17 congress in Denver, USA, and then exposed in a detailed position paper the successive year (Mehaffy, Porta, Rofè & Salingaros 2010). In that paper we have defined "main streets" as those streets that feature a global communication between urban areas, linking local places with their wider spatial, economic and social context. [15] In small villages and towns main streets are those that head out of the urban precinct towards adjacent villages and towns and further on to the larger regional space. Within cities, main streets are those that connect local places with other local places across significant portions of the city's fabric. The evolution of cities, during the phases of growth, has always been about generating less central streets from the more central, or main, followed by the gradual allotment and construction of the new street fronts on both sides. Major special urban functions like theatres, arenas, hospitals, city halls, libraries etc. are preferentially placed at main streets' crossings; ordinary functions like retail commerce, small offices and services also benefit from those prominent locations, but they may spill-off to residential districts along the more central of their service streets, or local main streets. Main streets are always the most central, and their crossings are usually 300–500 metres apart, so that we have termed this fundamental feature of traditional urbanism the 400-meters rule. Recent work conducted at UDSU, University of Strathclyde (Porta et al, in print) confirms that the 400-meters rule appears to inform all cities – both planned and self-organized – until the emergence of professional theories of urban design in late 19th and early 20th centuries.

Implications of the 400-meters rule for the theory and practice of urban design are many. One major implication is that we should not consider neighbourhoods as geographic entities anymore, and that basing our urban models on circles of 400 meters of radius on the assumption that they represent neighbourhoods, a never questioned norm of professional theories of urban design since Clarence Perry to the latest New Urbanist schemes, means throwing cities in the hyperspace of a lethal out-of-scale.

Disjointed Development: The potential of small plots to enable change and diversity gets inhibited if these are not controlled by different subjects. It is the diversity of subjects who exert control over small plots that enables change. Disjointed development is a process of spatial structure creation that subjects small plots to developmental paths that are autonomous from each other, though possibly under a shared agreement on basic principles. That autonomy may be expressed in different terms from case to case, including diversity of developers, owners, renters, and designers. Though disjointed development applies to the process of land development or regeneration at the design/creation phase, its consequences are all projected into the phase of post-design, enacting the dynamic of diversity emergence and informal participation that stands at the heart of plot-based, traditional urbanism. In other words, small plots must be coupled with disjointed development, i.e. plot control assigned plot-by-plot to different subjects, in order for informal change to start and keep happening.

In this sense, disjointed development is the reverse of conventional 'instant city' dynamics, which are based on making it as big as it can possibly be to take advantage of economies of scale. On the other hand, increasingly research and practice shows that the fragmentation of units of development fits particularly well the risk-sensible environment of the market in times of financial instability and economic downturn. If the basis of evidence on pros and cons of disjointed development in financial terms is still to a large extent a matter of research, nevertheless this principle appears to be crucial in terms of urban form and sociability of places.

3.3. Plot-Based Urbanism in Higher Education: Towards Local Urban Codes

The theory of urban seeding and the practice of plot-based urbanism have been the latest backbone of education in urban design at the University of Strathclyde, Glasgow, UK. The authors run a Masters in Urban Design course at the Department of Architecture, which is offered at the fifth year level of studies to students of Advanced Architectural Design and to others from a variety of backgrounds related to the disciplines of the built environment, such as planning, engineering, sociology or geography.

While we forward the reader to our website for accessing detailed information and documentation on the course (Porta & Romice 2010), it is important here to highlight its two main features that are prominently devoted to interpret the evolutionary nature of plot-based urbanism, i.e. morphometric analysis and Local Urban Code.

Morphometric analysis is a package of two analytical techniques aimed at the measurement of key spatial features of cities, one that focuses on street networks and one other that targets the spatial structure of blocks and street fronts. The outcomes of these two applications are set to inform directly the generation of a form-based code, i.e. a set of rules for the further development of urban spaces that in turn acts as guidance in the design of the final master plan.

The street network of the study area is modelled by means of a Multiple Centrality Assessment (MCA) approach based on Geographic Information System (GIS) and computer aided procedures of centrality calculations. Developed in recent years at UDSU (Porta, Latora & Strano 2010), this technique is a plain application of the network analysis of complex systems in nature, society or technology to phenomena characterized by spatial embedding (Boccalotti, Latora, Moreno, Chavez & Wang 2006). Building on a previous "Space Syntax" model (Hillier & Hanson 1984) but exploiting an entirely different computational engine, the package allows mapping centrality in urban streets, i.e. understanding what streets are more central and what are less central, depending only on their geometry and the way they are connected with each other in the system. The outcome of the procedure is a map of streets where streets are colour-coded in a blue-to-red grading expressing lower-to-higher centrality. This captures a profound meaning of the nature of urban streets which is deeply linked with city's formation in history and, especially, with the potential of streets to act today as social hot spots, or neighbourhood centres. This potential, for example, heavily contributes to the attractiveness of a street to retail

16 Student Sarah-Jane Laverick's work on street front design: small plots are clearly defined and different architectural solutions are quickly tested on each plot, all compatible with measures set in the Local Urban Code. Different and possibly opposite approaches to architectural design can and do coexist under the same structural norms stated in the Local Urban Code, which are based on the analysis of case studies selected from existent areas in the city of Glasgow. These norms are non-style-specific.

commerce and services, thus determining the level of self-surveillance and sociability of urban places. The analysis is normally conducted on different scenarios of street layout, including the current state and project alternatives, thus allowing students to raise evidence on how choices regarding one street have often unexpected consequences possibly far away from it, a typical behaviour of all kinds of complex systems.

In general terms, centrality correlates with land use intensity in terms of both population and employment (Wang, Antipova & Porta 2011), which impacts on real estate values and, as a consequence, on the form of street fronts. This link is tested on the ground in the course by means of a second analytical technique aimed at mapping the spatial structure of blocks and street fronts. Students organized in groups map out existent blocks in the study area and in Glasgow at large picking up cases that appear to represent all the different ways the city had been built in history. 'Bad' and 'good' cases are therefore investigated, measured and confronted, including for example Victorian tenement houses as much as post-war conventional high-rise tower blocks, or Edwardian suburbs of detached villas or cottages in plot. For each case spatial features are confronted with street centrality reported from the MCA analysis, thus visualizing this fundamental correlation in the specific reality of local districts.

All this analytical effort is not just aimed at increasing our knowledge of city functioning, but is strictly linked with the specific nature of our discipline as urban designers: taking action. This passage is ensured by means of the construction of a Local Urban Code. The Local Urban Code is a set of quantitative norms that are meant to be of reference in developing or regenerating the study area. Values such as percentage of built front, density of entrances, ground floor height, plot front width, plot size, plot compactness and several tens of others, are directly taken from the in-depth analysis of real blocks and street fronts illustrated above, therefore ensuring that decisions are taken with full and realistic awareness of their social and environmental consequences as proven after the examinations of parallel cases on the ground. The factor that drives this passage from existent cases to new designed cases is density. Cases in the analytical phase are grouped in categories depending on their density, and the same categories of density are used to frame the Local Urban Code that guide the future development or regeneration of the study area.

One thing is of utmost importance: the Local Urban Code does not deal with the architectural design of buildings. It is a specific concept in our course, and a crucial nature of our understanding of urban design, that there is a profound difference between the structure and the language of spaces that has to do with what is stable and general and what is changeable and specific, the former being the domain of urban design and the latter that of architecture. To proof this point in practice, at the end of the year students are immersed in a workshop experience where two architects well known for representing different and even opposite linguistic approaches (for example we invited Robert Adam and Gordon Murray) lead them to design single buildings as differently as they possibly can under the same norms set in the Local Urban Code. This difference in design culture expresses a wider difference in the management of autonomously developed small plots that would include developer and ownership forms of submission. [16]

4. URBAN SUSTAINABILITY

Plot-based urbanism is here advocated as an appropriate, responsive and sustainable form of development, because it is versatile and capable of minimising and spreading risk in conditions of adverse economies, it is conducive to informal participation, capacity building development of local capital, it has proven to be the most resilient form of urban development in time, and it is respectful to local character

We argue that plot-based urbanism is an approach that deserves consideration and development, because urban form and land use patterns are primary determinants of urban sustainability (Beatley 2000). This is paramount now at both local and global scale, for two main reasons:

1. Unprecedented urban growth is taking place especially in the developing countries of Asia, Africa, Latin America and Middle East. The urban population of developing countries will make up more than the 80 per cent of the urban population on planet Earth by year 2030. The urban population in Africa and Asia is expected to double between 2000 and 2030, with some 1.7 billion new urbanities in the next 20 years expected to be poor. New approaches to guide and support development that are not planning intensive and based on informal practices of traditional urbanism are urgently needed and conventional ones are no longer appropriate.

2. In the developed part of the world, which was already between 80 and 90 per cent urban at the turn of the millennium, the real challenge is about regenerating energy-intensive existing neighbourhoods in relation to both their housing stock and the urban model on which they are based. In the UK for example, the average urban density has dropped from 250 units and 1,500 people per hectare in 1900 to 35 units and about 80 people per hectare in 2005 (Power 2006), with the passage to a predominantly automobile dependent urbanization model. Throughout the Western world, ecological footprint consumption is between three to six times the current available rate of productive land, an unbalance allowed by the under consumption of developing countries (Frey & Yaneske 2007); appropriate urban development can help re-establish a fairer distribution, consumption and production of resources.

Planning for appropriate urban development is nowadays an imperative that, contrary to the past, can no longer afford mistakes; tolerance of aberrations ought to be reduced to a minimum simply because we no longer can afford the social, economic and environmental repercussions which would derive. Hence, urban development needs to be based upon carefully collected and interpreted evidence, no longer be left to ideology or trends. Urban development should be taught and practiced in an evidence-based manner, on the assumption that effects on the environment and its people can be monitored and modelled; the more precise the observation and evidence collected, the more tailored the outcomes of development. Future professionals must be taught to analyse, derive and design change to maximise environmental performance in terms of its impact on the ecological footprint, carbon emission, community building and place identity. The evidence-based approach to analysis and design should be at the core of the agenda for place making.

Evidence-based urban design should not be seen in juxtaposition to collaborative planning and participation of inhabitants in decision-making on urban change. Quite on the contrary, it is important to understand that planning – good planning – is the precondition for self-organization and informal participation to emerge and keep happening in time.

On the other hand, informal participation should not be seen in juxtaposition to formal participation approaches like Enquiry by Design or charrettes. We need both, as they deal with different and overlapping domains of urban change: the former has to do with post-design phase and the ordinary urban spaces, the latter mainly with the design phase and the extraordinary urban spaces.

Global and local challenges related with urbanism are today of such magnitude and nature that good planning, based on the "lost art of subdivision" must be re-established with urgency and cannot be deferred, with new relevance brought in this perspective to the public sector (Campbell 2010).

Trends are regarded as a first level global challenge to the environment as well as to the social and economic survival of our civilization: much of the future of our planet depends on how we will manage these challenges in the next three decades. Urban planners and designers cannot expect to deliver the same solutions over and over again and obtain different results: we need a new integrated discipline of urban space, a new structural approach that poses change (and therefore time) at the centre stage and acknowledges the complex multi-layered, multidisciplinary and inherently self-organized nature of urban phenomena.

In this paper we have named this different culture, recurring to an organic metaphor, urban seeding; we have outlined what are the conceptual basis of this culture highlighting the importance of time consciousness, adaptation and informal participation; we have then outlined several technical aspects of its many disciplinary facets grouping them under the notion of plot-based urbanism and looking at the history of cities to get inspiration and improve our knowledge. Finally, we have illustrated how these different culture and discipline can be taught to students with different backgrounds, including primarily students in architecture. "This is in fact starting to happen as Plot based urbanism attracts attention and makes it way among scholars, professionals and planning authorities internationally." (RRAAM, 2011)

All this should be seen as a first step towards good planning (whose content of novelty is here not of interest and consequently not debated), and therefore towards more diverse, vibrant, adaptable, democratic and in short human urban spaces. It is our only intent to open the ideas illustrated in this paper to reformulation across the widest possible discussion, in order to walk fast towards human and sustainable cities for our urban future.

It is essential that such different culture and discipline of urbanism are defined and developed in order to avoid gross mistakes and superficial misunderstandings that are seemingly pervasive in a media-oriented market of fashionable architectural image. The risk that concepts and goals of plot-based urbanism are quickly translated in very partial ready-made solutions by architects and planners is almost certainly taking over if a wider and deeper awareness does not emerge on its fundamental structural components. We clearly see the signs of such a new wave of pseudo-plot-based urbanism, i.e. just a latest version of a more general "valueless postmodern formalism" (Samuels, Panerai, Castex & Depaule 2004), beginning to spring out across magazines and academic work. [17]

17 *Master plan of the Expo Area for Milan World Exhibition 2015. Created by a pool of internationally renowned architects and academics including Jacques Herzog, Ricky Burdett, Stefano Boeri and William McDonough, this 'à-la-Java' design shows that plots have now captured the attention of world-class shape-makers. However, the rest of what constitutes a livable and adaptable urban structure, for example the human scale of blocks or the link between centrality of streets, plot and building types, does not appear to have played a significant role in this plan, putting at risk the subtle transition between the big event and the ordinary life of this part of Milan in the centuries to come (Boeri 2010).*

Footnotes

1 This paper is the result of passionate discussions among a group of people that includes, but is not limited to, the authors. Concepts and ideas have been shared and confronted by email and in person on many occasions and tested with students. In particular we want to thank Diarmaid Lawlor, who has animated the debate and set the opportunity to write this paper, as well as John Habraken, Michael Mehaffy, Kevin Thwaites, Yodan Rofè, Nikos Salingaros, Robert Adam, Sjoerd Soeters and Gian Luigi Maffei, who have directly contributed to the formation of these ideas in many ways. Also, we want to mention the endless discussions that we all within our unit of research at University of Strathclyde, the Urban Design Studies Unit (UDSU), have undertaken in the last three years about evolution in biology and urbanism, with special thanks to Emanuele Strano, Andrea Cardini and Eugenio Morello for their invaluable insight and support.

2 Levittown is a suburban low-density development realized in 1948 by the developer William Levitt in New York, USA. The development became the model for many such realizations that Mr Levitt and his company, Levitt & Sons Inc., realized across the United States after WWII. The model ultimately was popularly taken to epitomize the kind of single-family, residential and commercial developments for the lower middle class that we call now 'sprawl'. Pruitt-Igoe was an award-winning social housing project designed by architect Minoru Yamasaky and realized in Saint Louis, Missouri, USA, in 1955. The project followed the Le Corbusier principles of the Radiant City being constituted by 33 apartment buildings of eleven storeys of height located in a vast 'green' open area. In order to create "vertical neighbourhoods" buildings embedded a "service street" at any "anchor floor", the floor – one every three – where the lift stopped. Eventually the development, notwithstanding the high-rise building typology, did not go beyond a gross territorial density of 50 units per acre. Pruitt-Igoe started since its very completion to be stage for social problems of all sorts, ending up in a complete demolition which took place in 1972. The demolition event, broadcasted live in the whole USA, generated a large debate about the role that the spatial setting plays in shaping social behaviours and a first popular awareness of the shortcomings of the modern city. Pruitt-Igoe is still taken as a symbol of the failures of modern city planning as applied by celebrated masters of architectural theory and profession.

3 The popular meaning of suburbia refers to a mainly automobile-dependent, low-density, low-rise residential development located at commuting distance from any urban centre. This sprawled model of urbanization has been typically constituting the most of urbanization processes in the Western world across the 20th century. Recent studies have emphasized changes in the role and structure of suburbia after the passage to a post-industrial age (Garreau 1991), or its morphological character as related to that of urban centres (see especially the Urban Morphology Research Group, University of Birmingham, http://www.gees.bham.ac.uk/research/clusters/urbanmorphology/index.shtml).

4 Futurama was the largest architectural model ever constructed, spanning over 35,000 square feet, presented at New York World's Fair of 1939 and 1940. The model was produced and shown at the General Motors Pavilion, and represented the "city of the future" incarnating the principles of what we now would call an automobile-dependent out-of-scale techno-nightmare of International Style architecture, with plenty of gigantic glass-and-chromium high-rise buildings connected by endless streams of vehicles in motion on sky-passages. The whole World Exhibition was intended to be a 1:1 illustration of the magnificent future world in the motor-age, clearly influenced by the visions of modern architects such as Le Corbusier and Mies van der Rohe. Its impact on collective imaginary was profound and lasting, which evidently contributed driving the real development of cities during the boom after WWII.

References

J. Akbar, *Crisis in the Built Ennvironment: The Case of the Muslim City*, Singapore 1988.

C. Alexander, *A city is not a tree*. Architectural Forum, 122 (1), (Part I), 58–62, 1965.

C. Alexander, "Harmony Seeking Computation: A Science of Non-Classical Dynamics Based on the Progressive Evolution of the Larger Whole", *International Journal of Unconventional Computation*, in print.

C. Alexander, *The timeless way of building*, Oxford 1980.

D. Appleyard, *Livable streets*, Berkeley 1982.

F. Arneil-Walker, "Glasgow's New Towns", in P. Reed (Ed.), *Glasgow. The Forming of the City*, pp. 24–40, Edinburgh 1993.

D. Baird, M. Feeley, P. Russell & K. T. Wong, *Alterations in Scale: A Cartography of Urban Frameworks. Antiquity – New Urbanism*, University of Strathclyde, Department of Architecture. Glasgow: University of Strathclyde, 2010.

M. Barthélemy, "Spatial networks", Physics Reports, 499, pp. 1–101, 2011.

T. Beatley, *Green Urbanism: Learning from European Cities*, Washington DC, 2000.

S. Boccaletti, V. Latora, Y. Moreno, M. Chavez & D. Wang, "Complex Networks: Structure and Dynamics", in: *Physical Reports*, 424, pp. 175–308, 2006.

S. Boeri, *Expo Milano 2015_Presentation at BIE in Paris*. Retrieved 2010-12-September from Stefano Boeri Architetti: http://www.stefanoboeriarchitetti.net/?p=3245, 2010.

P. Calthorpe & W. Fulton, *The Regional City: Planning for the End of Sprawl*. Washington DC, 2001.

K. Campbell, "Briefing: Making Massive Small Change", in: *Urban Design and Planning* (163), pp. 3–6, 2010.

G. Caniggia & G. L. Maffei, *Architectural Composition and Building Typology: Interpreting Basic Building*, Florence 2001.

M. Carmona, T. Heath, T. Oc & S. Tiesdell,

Public Places – Urban Spaces: A Guide to Urban Design, Oxford 2003.

J. Cockburn, *Tenement: A Novel of Glasgow Life*, Edinburgh 1925.

M. R. Conzen, *Alnwick, Northumberland: A Study in Town-Plan Analysis*, London 1960.

M. R. Conzen, "Morphogenesis, Morphological Regions and Secular Human Agency in the Historic Townscape", in: D. Denecke & G. Shaw, *Urban Historical Geography: Recent Progress in Britain and Germany*, pp. 253–272, Cambridge 1988.

Le Corbusier, *Vers une architecture*, Paris 1923.

G. Cullen, *Townscape*, Cambridge, Massachusetts, 1965.

A. Cuthbert, "Urban Design: Requiem for an Era: Review and Critique of the Last 50 years", in: *Urban Design International*, 12, pp. 177–223, 2007.

English Partnership and Housing Corporation, *Urban Design Compendium*, London 2000.

H. Frey, *Designing the City: Towards a More Sustainable Urban Form*, London 1999.

H. Frey & P. Yaneske, *Visions of Sustainability: Cities and Regions*, Abingdon, 2007.

J. Habraken, *Palladio's Children: Essays on Everyday Environment and the Architect*, (J. Teicher, Ed.) New York 2005.

J. Habraken, *The Structure of the Ordinary: Form and Control in the Built Environment*, (J. Teicher, Ed.) Cambridge 2000.

L. Hart, J. Hooi, O. Romice & S. Porta, *Under the Microscope: 20 Small Towns in Scotland*, Glasgow 2010.

B. Hillier, *Space is the Machine: A Configurational Theory of Architecture*, Cambridge 1996.

B. Hillier & J. Hanson, *The Social Logic of Space*, Cambridge 1984.

E. Howard, *Garden Cities of To-morrow*, London 1902.

J. Innes, & D. Booher, "Consensus-Building as Role-Playing and Bricolage: Toward a Theory of Collaborative Planning, in: *Journal of the American Planning Association*, 65 (1), pp. 9-26, 1999.

A. Jacobs & D. Appleyard, "Toward an Urban Design Manifesto", in: *Journal of the American Planning Association*, 53 (1), pp. 112-120, 1987.

J. Jacobs, *The Death and Life of Great American Cities*, New York 1961.

M. Jenks & R. Burgess, *Compact Cities: Sustainable Urban Form for Developing Countries*, London 2000.

J. P. Kleihues, *International Building Exhibition Berlin 1987: Examples of a New Architecture*, Berlin 1987.

A. Krieger, & W. Lennerz, *Towns and Townmaking Principles: Andres Duany and Elizabeth Plater-Zyberck, Architects*, New York 1991.

A. Laird, *Hyndland: Edwardian Glasgow Tenement Suburb*, Glasgow 1997.

K. Lynch, *The Image of the City*, Cambridge 1960.

J.-F. Lyotard, *The Postmodern Condition: A Report on Knowledge*, Manchester 1979.

S. McGlynn, G. Smith, A. Alcock, P. Murrain & I. Bentley, *Responsive Environments: A Manual for Designers*, Oxford 1985.

M. Mehaffy, S. Porta, Y. Rofè & N. Salingaros, "Urban Nuclei and the Geometry of Streets: The 'Emergent Neighborhoods' Model", in: *Urban Design International*, 15 (1), pp. 22-46, 2010.

O. Newman, *Defensible Space: Crime Prevention Through Environmental Design*, New York 1973.

P. Newman & J. Kenworthy, *Sustainability and Cities: Overcoming Automobile Dependence*, Washington DC 1999.

S. Porta, "What if Icarus Chooses the Labyrinth?",in: S. Porta (Ed.), *Il riscatto dei quartieri sociali. Una questione anche disciplinare*, Milan 2006.

S. Porta & O. Romice, *MSc in Urban Design.* (University of Strathclyde) Retrieved 2010-4-September from Urban Design Studies Unit: http://www.udsu-strath.com/section/2-education/2-1-mscud/

S. Porta, P. Crucitti & V. Latora, "The Network Analysis of Urban Streets. A Primal Approach", in: *Environment and Planning B, Planning and Design* (33), 705–725, 2006.

S. Porta, V. Latora & E. Strano, "Networks in Urban Design: Six Years of Research in Multiple Centrality Assessment", in: E. Estrada, M. Fox, D. Higham & G. L. Oppo (Eds.), *Network Science: Complexity in Nature and Technology*, pp. 107–130, London 2010.

S. Porta, V. Latora, F. Wang & S. Scellato, "Street Centrality and Densities of Retail and Services in Bologna, Italy." *Environment and Planning B, Planning and Design*, 36, pp. 450–465, 2009.

S. Porta, O. Romice, J. A. Maxwell, P. Russell, D. Baird, "Alterations in Scale: Patterns of Change in Main Street Networks Across Time and Space", *Urban Studies*, in print.

A. Power, "The Changing Face of Cities", *Environment on the edge*, Cambridge 2006.

P. Reed, "The Tenement City", in: P. Reed (Ed.), *Glasgow. The forming of the city*, pp. 105–129, Edinburgh 1993.

RRAAM, Concept Ontwikkelstrategie Almere Oosterwold, available at: http://www.duurzaamalmere.nl/wp-content/uploads/downloads/2011/12/LR-Almere-Oosterwold-11-sept_2.pdf, 2011, visited in February 2014.

I. Samuels, "Architectural Practice and Urban Morphology", in: T. Slater (Ed.), *The Built Form of Western Cities*, Leicester 1990.

I. Samuels, P. Panerai, J. Castex & J.-C. Depaule, *Urban Forms: The Death and Life of the Urban Block*, Oxford 2004.

T. Slater, *Medieval Composite Plan Towns in England: Evidence from Bridgnorth, Shropshire*. University of Birmingham, School of Geography. Birmingham 1988.

The Urban Task Force, *Towards an Urban Renaissance*, London 1999.

K. Thwaites, S. Porta, O. Romice & M. Greaves, *Urban Sustainability through Environmental Design: Approaches to Time-People-Place Responsive Urban Spaces*, London 2008.

S. Tobriner, *The Genesis of Noto, an Eighteenth-Century Sicilian City*, London 1982.

F. Wang, A. Antipova & S. Porta, "Street Centrality and Land Use Intensity in Baton Rouge", Louisiana. *Journal of Transport Geography*, in print.

F. Worsdall, *The Tenement, a Way of Life: A Social, Historical and Architectural Study of Housing in Glasgow*, Edinburgh 1979.

Autoren / Authors

Harald Bodenschatz has been Professor for Sociology of Planning and Architecture at the TU Berlin and is now Associate Fellow of the Center for Metropolitan Studies at the TU Berlin. He is partner of the planning office Gruppe DASS. He studied sociology, political science, psychology and economy in Munich and Berlin. He has also been teaching in Aachen, Rio de Janeiro and Lima. He is a founding member of the Council of European Urbanism (C.E.U.).

Ben Bolgar is Senior Director at the Prince's Foundation for Building Community in London. His fields include the collation of applied theory and leading new building and community regeneration projects. He has studied architecture at Heriot-Watt University in Edinburgh and the University of Notre Dame in South Bend, Indiana.

Matthew Carmona is Professor of Planning and Urban Design at the Bartlett School of Planning, University College London. He has studied architecture at the University of Nottingham. He has previously lectured at the University of Nottingham and before that worked as a researcher at Strathclyde and Reading Universities and as an architect in practice. He is European Associate Editor for the *Journal of Urban Design*.

Norman Garrick is Associate Professor of Civil Engineering at the University of Connecticut and Director of UCONN's new Center for Smart Transportation. He is a Board Member of the Congress for the New Urbanism. He has studied civil engineering at the University of the West Indies in Trinidad and at Purdue University in West Lafayette, Indiana.

Michael Hebbert is Professor of Town Planning at the Bartlett School, University College London, Professor Emeritus of the University of Manchester, and a member of MARC, the Manchester Architecture Research Centre. He studied history and geography at Oxford and Reading universities and formerly taught at Oxford Polytechnic and the London School of Economics. He is editor of the journal *Planning Perspectives*.

Christoph Mäckler is Professor of Urban Design at the Faculty of Architecture and Civil Engineering at the University of Technology in Dortmund (TU Dortmund). He is founding director of the German Institute for Civic Art (Deutsches Institut für Stadtbaukunst). He studied architecture in Aachen and holds the architectural office Professor Christoph Mäckler Architekten at Frankfurt am Main.

Sergio Porta is Professor of Urban Design, Head of Department and Director of the Urban Design Studies Unit at the Department of Architecture, University of Strathclyde, Glasgow. He has studied architecture at the Politecnico di Milano. He has also been teaching and researching at UC Berkeley and at Murdoch University in Perth.

Ombretta Romice is Senior Lecturer in Urban Design at the Department of Architecture, University of Strathclyde in Glasgow. She is also President of IAPS, the International Association for People-Environment Studies. She studied architecture at the Politecnico di Torino.

Wolfgang Sonne is Professor of History and Theory of Architecture at the Faculty of Architecture and Civil Engineering at the University of Technology in Dortmund (TU Dortmund). He is founding co-director of the German Institute for Civic Art (Deutsches Institut für Stadtbaukunst). He studied art history and archaeology in Munich, Paris and Berlin and has previously taught at the ETH Zurich and the University of Strathclyde in Glasgow.